YOUR LIFE,
GOD'S HOME

YOUR LIFE, GOD'S HOME

&

Knowing the Joy of
His Presence

NANCIE CARMICHAEL

CROSSWAY BOOKS • WHEATON, ILLINOIS
A DIVISION OF GOOD NEWS PUBLISHERS

Your Life, God's Home

Copyright © 1998 by Nancie Carmichael

Published by Crossway Books
　　　　a division of Good News Publishers
　　　　1300 Crescent Street
　　　　Wheaton, Illinois 60187

Cover photo: The Stock Market

Cover design: Cindy Kiple

First printing 1998

Printed in the United States of America

ISBN 1-58134-017-6

Scripture is taken from the *Holy Bible,* New King James Version, unless otherwise identified. Copyright © 1982, Thomas Nelson, Inc. Used by permission.

Scripture references marked NLT are taken from the *Holy Bible,* New Living Translation, copyright © 1996. Used by permission of Tyndale House Publishers, Inc., Wheaton, Ill., 60189. All rights reserved.

Scripture quotations taken from the *Revised Standard Version* are identified RSV. Copyright 1946, 1953 © 1971, 1973 by the Division of Christian Education of the National Council of Churches in the USA.

Scripture quotations taken from the King James Version are identified KJV.

Library of Congress Cataloging-in-Publication Data
Carmichael, Nancie.
　　Your life : God's home : knowing the joy of his presence /
Nancie Carmichael.
　　　p.　　cm.
　　Includes bibliographical references.
　　ISBN 0-58134-017-6 (alk. paper)
　　1. Spiritual life—Christianity.　2. Presence of God.　3. Carmichael,
Nancie.　4. Temple of God.　I. Title.
BV4501.2.C3157　　1998
248.4—dc21　　　　　　　　　　　　　　　98-19635
　　　　　　　　　　　　　　　　　　　　　　　　　　CIP

06		05		04		03		02		01		00		99		98
15	14	13	12	11	10	9	8	7	6	5	4	3	2	1

77220

To my sweet William
whom I love and respect with all my heart:
Thank you for holding my feet to the ground,
making this book possible!

And to my wonderful children
who believed in the message of this book
in spite of my self-doubt.
May your houses for God be
forever filled with His joy and peace.

"The work is great, because the temple
is not for man but for the LORD God."
—1 CHRONICLES 29:1

CONTENTS

Acknowledgments   ix

Introduction   11

1   The Foundation—Hidden Strength   15

2   Measuring Up—Building According to His Plan   31

3   Heartwood—My Life, a Gift   45

4   Framing—Life-Shaping Choices   63

5   The Bearing Wall —Testing the Choices   79

6   Infrastructure—House Comes Alive   95

7   Windows in My House—My Perspective   109

8   Doors in My House—Access to Rooms   125

9   Decorating—Meaning in the Mundane   141

10 Remodeling My House—Time for Change   159

11 House Beautiful—A Life of Value   181

Notes   201

ACKNOWLEDGMENTS

This book has been a long time in the making. Heartfelt thanks to Lane and Ebeth Dennis, publishers of Crossway, for their encouragement and affirmation, and to editor Lila Bishop for her invaluable assistance.

I am grateful to my treasured brothers and sisters for caring about my heart-and-soul book. (I know they are relieved not to have me thrusting portions of unfinished manuscript at them!) I am so thankful for the encouragement of extended family and friends. Their presence, their words have been "life" to me. I am blessed with amazingly wonderful and faithful friends, but I must extend special thanks to Bonnie Hoerner and Susan Berube for their initial reading of the oh-so-rough manuscript and their honest critiques.

I'll always be grateful to Lynn Vanderzalm for her keen insight, wisdom, and friendship. And to the "Shell Ring Group"—Pat and Connie Clements, Gene and Marylou Habecker, Bob and Joan Rhoden. Thanks for the laughter, tears, and prayers!

INTRODUCTION

It's been said that what is most personal is most universal, and this is a personal book. Using house as a metaphor for your life, I bring you into my own "house"—my life—and with you, try to understand what it means to be a "house for God." This book is meant to be read reflectively. Don't rush through it. You may wish to jot down your own thoughts in the space provided at the end of each chapter.

Physical houses have function, design, and unique settings. What is your house like? Is it a large place that makes a statement? Or is it a more simple, basic shelter? Is it one open to others or more private? And at what stage of building is your house? Is it now under construction, or do you need to do some restructuring?

You, too, have a unique purpose as you let God become more and more at home in your life. Think of it—to be His house, His dwelling place in the world. It is an awesome thought.

You and I have been given the wondrous—and sometimes painful—gift of life. No one has a life exactly like yours nor like mine. Our lives are shaped by our heritage, our environment, by choices we and others make; and each life has unique gifts and frailties. Each of us own certain joys, sorrows, hopes, and dreams. And each of us has the potential to live with God-given purpose, knowing that life is a gift from God to be gratefully received and generously shared.

The key to constructing a house for God is to allow the Chief Builder to do His work in us. God is the foundation, His Word the plumb line or measuring stick for our lives, and Jesus Christ is the cornerstone. With our invitation, Jesus makes something of beauty and meaning out of who we are.

Oswald Chambers said in the early part of this century, "Continually restate to yourself what the purpose of your life is. The destined end of man is not happiness, nor health, but holiness. Nowadays we have far too many affinities; we are dissipated with them—right, good, noble affinities which will yet have their fulfillment, but in the meantime God has to atrophy them. The one thing that matters is whether a man will accept the God who will make him holy. At all costs a man must be rightly related to God."[1]

Affinities is an old English word for ties, or relationships. The most important affinity we can have is with our Maker and Lord. His plans for each of us are good, and when He is at the center of our lives, there is peace, purpose, and wholeness. But I believe there is no way to live a life for God these days without purposeful intention. Now, more even than when Oswald Chambers wrote these words, our times are difficult, invasive. There are many "affinities" calling to each of us, begging for definition in our lives. But if I am to be defined as a dwelling place for God—a "house for God," I must learn from my Father, stay close to Him and ask Him into the very core of my being, seeking wisdom from His Word. And He does give it. And, yes, it takes time to be holy.

What does it actually take to build a strong, wonderful house? My husband, Bill, grew up with the sights and sounds of building, and to this day he loves the smell of freshly sawn lumber because it brings good memories of working beside his father, watching him, helping him build. Bill learned much from his father about building, and this knowledge helped him build the house that we live in today.

As I considered the metaphor of crafting my own "house for God," I have reflected on the actual building of the house we live in today. Bill told me, "What my father taught me about building not only has been essential information for building our house, but it has also been a graphic example for life's important lessons. There are very clear principles of building that I needed to follow in order to build a good, strong house for our family."

There are principles for building a good, strong life for God as well.

So, please . . . come into my house.

One

⁂

THE
FOUNDATION

⁂

Nevertheless the solid foundation of God stands, having this seal:
"The Lord knows those who are His," and, "Let everyone who names
the name of Christ depart from iniquity."

—2 TIMOTHY 2:19

Twenty years ago in the dry heat of August, the foundation for our house was finally completed. We were building the house of our dreams for our growing young family in the Cascade Mountains of Oregon near the magnificent Three Sisters mountains that the old settlers called Faith, Hope, and Charity.

Bill said, "Putting in the foundation was the first big step in actually building our house. It was absolutely essential that our foundation be placed on solid ground—on bedrock. Loose fill just would not do. The foundation had to be wide enough and deep enough to support the structure. The concrete had to be a certain consistency and contain enough rock to sustain our entire house."

He went on to tell me, "I knew I had to do a good job on the foundation because it provides the support and undergirding for our house. Everything must be exact. I have seen that when a house burns down, virtually everything is destroyed except the foundation. Most homes rebuilt after a fire use the same foundation as before, so it became very clear to me: The foundation is the most permanent and lasting part of any structure. I had to do it right—do it well."

MY FOUNDATION: FAITH IN GOD

> *The righteous has an everlasting foundation.*
>
> – PROVERBS 10:25

A foundation shapes and defines the house that grows from it. My life is shaped by many factors, but as I consider the foundation of my own life—what holds me—it is my faith in God. This is perhaps the single most important factor of my life. I cannot say that I have never doubted nor wavered. I have. And yet I have become increasingly aware that my spiritual "home"—my base of support—is belief in a personal God.

> *Three things are to be looked to in a building:*
> *that it stand on the right spot;*
> *that it be securely founded;*
> *that it be successfully executed.* [1]
>
> – GOETHE

Our oldest son Jon and his wife, Brittni, have just built their first house. Jon eagerly showed me around the construction site one day. I tiptoed around the rocks and mud as I hurried to keep up with him, somewhat in awe. It didn't seem so long ago that I sat on the bleachers at a Little League game, watching my towheaded firstborn play baseball. Jon and Brittni's house is on a narrow lot on a steep hillside in Portland with a wonderful view of the river and beyond to Mt. Hood. The foundation had to be dug deep and massive in order to support the tri-level house that rises straight up like a tree house.

This house, I thought with amazement, *is going to be beautiful.*

Advice and suggestions kept occurring to me; however, I was silent, simply admiring this rough work in progress. It had been difficult to visualize the house until now; but with the foundation poured and set, I could see the possibilities.

Make sure of your foundation, son, I half-prayed, half-advised under my breath as I admired his new place. I thought of our house, the house where Jon grew up in Sisters, Oregon, 140 miles away from Portland. Our house has a good foundation, Bill assures me, dug well below the frost line. The house—a tall, rambling affair my husband built with the help of his father—stands among giant Ponderosa pines. Through the center of the house rises a massive rock fireplace made from gray-blue granite we found one summer day after a hilarious and memorable search. The fireplace is set on a concrete pad over two feet thick, reinforced by steel rods. The pad rests on lava rock.

Just as the foundation shaped and secured our physical house, so our spiritual foundation has the potential to shape our lives, setting us on an unfolding journey of discovery and mystery. As Dag Hammarskjöld wrote in *Markings:*

> I don't know Who-or-what put the question. . . . I don't even remember answering. But at some moment I did answer Yes to Someone-or-Something, and from that hour I was certain that existence is meaningful and that, therefore, my life, in self-surrender, had a goal.[2]

A spiritual foundation determines the shape, the goal for the rest of our lives. Oswald Chambers wrote of it: "No love of the natural heart is safe unless the human heart has been satisfied by God first."

How did I come to have a foundation of faith? Do I believe because my parents believed—is it simply a family tradition, or is the foundation my own? Certainly, the lives of my mother and father affected me. Their spiritual quests were not mine; yet mine began with theirs. It is a process, this building business—layer upon layer, stone upon stone through the years. But the foundation—what I build my life on—is what I rest my very existence on in the shifting sands of this life.

I was born to parents who were committed Christians, and I never knew life without faith in God as an integral part of life. The danger in growing up with this is to take the foundation for granted—that simply because my parents were lovers of God, I would be, too.

And yet my parents were not always Christians. As I've thought about my spiritual foundation, I became curious. What were my parents' lives like before they became Christians? What practical difference did it make in their lives to have a spiritual foundation? Perhaps you, too, grew up with Christian parents. It may give you insight to trace your family history to see where your spiritual foundations began. Or perhaps you are starting fresh in your own life, establishing new foundations.

Since neither of my parents are living, I had to make phone calls and contacts to people who knew them years ago, digging out old letters. I found out that for my father, it began in Lignite, North Dakota, fifteen years before I was born. Lignite was a small town then, about 217 people. My father's family lived some distance from town. My grandfather Gabriel was a Lutheran minister who died at the age of thirty-nine of a ruptured appendix, leaving my grandmother Henny and six young children. Henny was known for her hospitality, and there was always company, extra people staying at her house. After Gabriel died, she remarried and had three more children, making a total of nine. My father was the second oldest son in the family.

In 1932 a pretty nineteen-year-old woman named Catherine Strumswald from Minot, North Dakota, came to Lignite and began holding street meetings. When interest and crowds grew, she rented the Congregational church and began having regular meetings. Many in the town became Christians, including my father. I can only imagine the curiosity. My father, a handsome, blue-eyed twenty-one-year-old, his brothers, and my father's best friend Clint must have been intrigued by this pretty young preacher.

Clint, who started first grade with my father in 1918, recently told me what my father was like before he committed his life to Christ. He had been confirmed as a child, but over the years he'd rebelled and gone his own way. "Gunder and I were in a pretty rowdy gang—drinking, doing a lot of cutting up," he said. It's hard to imagine, as I only knew my father as a gentle and quiet man who visited sick neighbors and was at church every time the doors were open.

By the time my father was twenty-one, he had already seen the harsh side of life with the death of his father and hard financial times. And then his stepfather, an emotionally troubled man, committed suicide. Perhaps the appeal of partying was one way my father forgot the troubles at home. When my father walked to the altar at the church, it was not a casual step for him; it meant radical change. His religion became personal, and from that moment, my father had new priorities—lasting ones that helped shape the foundation of my life to this day. After his conversion, his life centered around personal holiness, Bible study, prayer, and going to church.

My mother's story of coming to Christ was different but no less dramatic. Her spiritual awakening began in 1934 in Wolf Point, Montana, near the Indian reservation. She was a twenty-four-year-old red-haired woman with a lively sense of humor. She moved to town with her two-year-old daughter and her mother, who helped care for the little girl. My mother was a hairdresser in town—a good one, too. She'd had her heart broken, it was whispered, by a man who'd loved her and left her; and in those days, it was a great shame—not to mention financially challenging—to be a single mother.

One day as my grandmother baby-sat for her dark-haired little granddaughter, a local pastor knocked at her door and invited her to church. She accepted his invitation, and soon after, she became a

Christian. She began praying for her two children—her daughter Harriet and her son Kenneth (who lived and worked in a nearby town). Kenneth became a Christian first, and then he began praying for his younger sister Harriet. It took some convincing for my mother to come to church, because she was afraid that becoming a Christian would mean she'd have to be an "old fuddy-duddy," as she put it. But one night Kenneth had been asked to speak, and Harriet decided to come and hear her older brother whom she adored. It is only now that I understand the strong bond between my mother and her brother. He was not just her brother; he was her spiritual father and mentor.

That night something dramatic happened to Harriet. At the close of the service, she walked to the front as an indication that she intended to follow Christ. There was weeping and laughter and joy as the little family hugged each other around the altar. She was saved. *Saved* may be a somewhat old-fashioned word, but it describes what happened to my mother. In spite of her fun-loving front, Harriet had been brokenhearted by life, and that night she was rescued by a love that would never let her go. From that time on, my mother began a love relationship with a personal God found in the pages of the Bible—a love that helped shape the foundation of my own life.

As I read worn, yellowed letters and talk to old friends about their conversions, I am struck by the wholeheartedness of their experiences. Perhaps it was the times. It was the Great Depression, and they had very little. And when they did come to God, it was to an altar. My mother confessed years later that when she became a Christian, she burned all her poetry and writing.

"Why?" I asked, aghast.

"I don't know—it was just something I felt I had to do. I wanted to give everything that I was, everything I had to God and start fresh."

A gospel song from that era pointedly asks, "Is your all on the altar of sacrifice laid? Your heart, does the Spirit control? You can only be blest and have peace and sweet rest, as you yield Him your body and soul."[3]

Undoubtedly there was some legalism in the holiness movement, but the overriding theme in "getting saved" was of no compromise with the world. It reminds me of principles for building a foundation. There can be no compromise: The foundation must be based on bedrock for the building to endure. Faith in Christ changed my parents, each of them in individual ways.

How does one establish a foundation? While I did not have as dramatic a conversion as my parents, I still had to establish my own foundation. And I have discovered that as I go through each phase of life, as I enter new places, I must again make Jesus Lord of that place. I will discuss more about this in later chapters. But I am continually reminded of my foundation throughout life, knowing it must be mine. And your foundation must be one you establish. A wise man once told me, "God has no grandchildren—only children."

Convinced of the Foundation

We know too much, and are convinced of too little. . . .[4]

—T. S. ELIOT

Faith is ours only when it is personal. Our hearts must become involved. We must understand: We need Him; we are lost without Him. It is possible to go through life, do all the right things, and not have a foundation established. Proverbs 4:23 says, "Keep your heart with all diligence, for out of it spring the issues of life." Becoming convinced of our foundation is an affair of the heart.

Jesus said, "Where your treasure is, there your heart will be also" (Matt. 6:21). We must give our whole heart—our love, our treasure—to the same one who held Edward Mote, who penned these words over a hundred years ago: "My hope is built on nothing less than Jesus' blood and righteousness;/I dare not trust the sweetest frame, but wholly lean on Jesus' name./ On Christ the solid rock I stand, all other ground is sinking sand!"[5]

This faith—this foundation—is a gift of God. We cannot earn nor manufacture it. The new birth is a mystery that arises from acceptance of Jesus Christ and His work on the cross.

My Foundation . . . the Shape of an Altar

It was at an altar at Vacation Bible School where I came forward to announce my intention to accept Christ. It was at family altar as a child that my father would pray for any family member who needed prayer.

At an altar Bill and I promised before God that we would be true to one another for life. It was at an altar where Bill and I dedicated each of our five children to God, promising Him that we would do our best to raise them to know God.

It was at an altar where Bill was ordained, and we joined hands and accepted a Bible and a charge to "preach the Word."

My foundation is made up of sacred commitments and vows and solemn promises to ideals far bigger and grander than anything I could conceptualize. This foundation—its chief cornerstone Christ Jesus and His work on the cross—is built on faith and reinforced by real-life examples of many before me.

An unknown author described it this way:

> *Upon a life I did not live; Upon a death I did not die*
> *Upon another's life, another's death; I risk my soul eternally.*

I have become convinced of my foundation through time, through testing its truths, and through faith by hearing God's Word. I have become convinced by realizing everything else the world has to offer—its sparkling wisdom, its temporary gifts and trends—is temporary, and God alone is worth trusting.

Hidden Strength

The thing about a foundation is that even though it is essential to the success of a house, a foundation is not what is most immediately noticeable. It is hidden; yet its influence becomes evident to all. One needn't go around talking about it—making big signs with arrows that say, "FOUNDATION HERE." It simply becomes obvious over a matter of time as erosion and the storms of life reveal the strength of the foundation.

I hope that the foundation of my life is evident to those around me. I hope others don't just see a religious person, but someone (in spite of my faults and shortcomings) who is *weighted,* grounded in something bigger than herself. Jesus said, "Anyone who listens to my teaching and obeys me is wise, like a person who builds a house on solid rock. Though the rain comes in torrents and the floodwaters rise and the winds beat against that house, it won't collapse, because it is built on rock" (Matt. 7:24-25 NLT).

The foundation keeps a house, especially when storms come. Jesus did not say, "In the unlikely event of a storm . . . " He said, "The floods came, and the winds blew and beat on that house; and it did not fall, for it was founded on the rock" (Matt. 7:25). He also said, "In the world you *will* have much tribulation; but be of good cheer, I have overcome the world" (John 16:33, italics mine). Being exposed to storms in life is part of being human.

Having a foundation meant security even in the worst of times for my friend, Virginia Phillips, who was widowed in her thirties with eight children under sixteen. She told me, "I learned I could only depend on God. I had to wait for everything. We had a $10,000 insurance policy and were $8,000 in debt. God brought me to the penny what I needed every month." She later married Joshua, a family counselor, and both of them went on to work in the areas of adoption, racial reconciliation, and family counseling. Virginia has lived through difficult days and has come out on the other side to wonderful, productive years and through it all, proved her foundation.

Having this foundation may mean a "hidden" strength that holds you through bumps in marriage as you work through them to better days. It may mean the unspoken commitment that keeps you to important promises you've made, and you stay with it week after week, even though results are not immediately evident. It may mean the dogged determination to keep praying for positive direction for a family member, even though it may not look positive at the moment. I think more than anything, though, a foundation of faith in God is to live day by ordinary day, knowing your life really does have purpose and destiny. You can trust Him as you rest upon the fact of His existence, knowing He is working things together for your good. "But God's truth stands firm like a foundation stone with this inscription: 'The Lord knows those who are his'" (2 Tim. 2:19 NLT).

Built for Better Things

> *No house should ever be on any hill or on anything. It should be of the hill, belonging to it. So hill and house could live together, each the happier for the other.*[6]
>
> — FRANK LLOYD WRIGHT

Not far from here is a new house that intrigues me. I am told that its owner lived in an identical house in another part of the country and liked it so much that he built one just like it here. It is an attractive house, but somehow it doesn't look right. It looks as if it belongs in an urban subdivision, not on the edge of a mountain meadow. The house has a rock facade and steep staircase, and the foundation appears as if designed for a split level to fit a hillside lot. But the lot, even though it has a wonderful view, is flat. The house does not fit the lot.

You and I are destined for greater things than just to fill up space here on earth. God has a design for each of our lives—a design that "fits the lot" where we will thrive. As Augustine wrote, within each of us is a God-shaped vacuum that only He can fill. For His pleasure, Scripture says, we are created (Rev. 4:11 KJV). God is the only one I can trust to lay the right foundation for my life, because He knows my real purpose. As He said to Job, "Where were you when I laid the foundation of the earth? Tell me, if you have understanding. Who determined its measurements—surely you know! Or who stretched the line upon it? On what were its bases sunk, or who laid its cornerstone, when the morning stars sang together, and all the sons of God shouted for joy?" (Job 38:4-7 RSV).

Calvin Miller wrote in *Walking with the Saints*:

> How often we err when we speak of "accepting Christ." It is a kind of statement that puts God's indwelling Son at the mercy of our caprice. Who are we to accept Christ or speak of it as though by accepting him, humanity does him a favor? . . . The coming of Christ into our lives is an issue of surrender and opening our lives. Our many quarreling selves become one in salvation. . . . Only when Christ comes in do we discover our own definition and why we are in the world. . . . We are saved from living the undefined life.[7]

My Cornerstone

The New England poet, Edna St. Vincent Millay, invited with wry wit:

> *Safe upon the solid rock the ugly houses stand:*
> *Come and see my shining palace built upon the sand!*[8]

It is tempting to try to build a shining palace. But no matter how gorgeous and well equipped it is, if it isn't built on the Cornerstone and founded on the Rock, it won't last. The temptation is subtle but stubborn: "This is my life. I can do what I want!"

I remember a vivid moment in my early teens. I was daydreaming of what I was going to do when I grew up, and I thought: *The world is mine for the taking. Anything is possible! I can dream big dreams, because they just may come true!* I had big plans for my life.

Not long ago I was alone, walking and praying and reflecting on dreams of youth and on my dreams now, and how different they are from each other. Midlife has brought me an awareness of my fragility, of how rapidly time is passing. *How my perspective has changed,* I thought, *from a sense of invincibility to weakness; yet now in the weakness, I understand my real security.*

As I was walking, I had a strong sense of God's presence. I had been studying the Bible, and its truths seemed so vibrant, so real to me that I had an unshakable conviction that anything could happen to me, and I would be safe in God. My foundation was sure. The Cornerstone, Jesus Christ, was holding it all together. *My life has been so blessed,* I thought, *knowing God; having the husband, children, and extended family that I have; being in my church and community; having friends who laugh with me, pray for me, and tell me the truth. So,* I reasoned, *anything could happen, and God would be there. Anything. He is my foundation; He is able, mighty to save.*

Later that week something happened to one of my children that deeply disappointed me, and I was left reeling. "God," I agonized, "I said anything could happen to me, not to him."

As I look back to this experience almost a year ago, it illustrates to me in a personal way what foundation means: Even though I didn't have immediate answers or assurances that everything would work out well, as I held onto my faith in God, I was held and secured. And the child in question is now doing well.

Yes, there have been storms in my life—the deaths of both of my parents, financial reversal, serious illness, personal disappointment—but through it all, my foundation holds. Life will come at us full-force if we live long enough. Even if we have this foundation of faith, will we face loss, difficulties? Yes, often. Even with this foundation of faith, will we have questions? Certainly. Will we face challenges beyond our capabilities? Of course! But through all of it, I have learned that my foundation stands firm, and as I look back and ahead, I am comforted to know that I am held, and all that I commit to Him is safe in His hands. It will be for you, too.

> For in the time of trouble He shall hide me in His pavilion; In the secret place of His tabernacle He shall hide me; He shall set me high upon a rock.
>
> —PSALM 27:5

Years ago before concrete foundations, builders relied upon the age-old intricate art of placing stones in positions and order so they would hold together. The stone at the corner of two walls that united them was called the "cornerstone." It was the stone built into one corner of the foundation as the actual starting point of a building. Jesus Christ is the cornerstone of my faith—and I pray He will be my children's cornerstone, too.

And now my children are building. As I walked around Jon and Brittni's new house, I thought of all that was going into their spiritual foundation as well, and I thank God that they know and trust Him in these rapidly changing days.

Times are different now from our parents' era, and we face different challenges. We have much materially and every other way. We have many options as to what should be our foundation. We can "add" faith to our lives as we add a piece of furniture or a life insurance policy. It is tempting to have the world and Jesus, too, fitting Him into our lives—except for the fact that a house can have only one foundation: "Let each one take heed how he builds on it. For no other foundation can anyone lay than that which is laid, which is Jesus Christ" (1 Cor. 3:10-11).

That is why the foundation of faith is, as E. Stanley Jones wrote, the divine Yes. It is the answer we give Him when faced with the basic question: "Do you trust Me?" and I say, "Yes . . . be my foundation." Because without God, there is a vast emptiness, an aching void, the God-shaped vacuum. But knowing the One True Foundation is a security that goes deep. In our inevitable human search for meaning, if we honestly seek Him, we will find Him—the solid rock against which you and I can build our lives.

WHAT IS YOUR FOUNDATION?

❧ Consider the analogy of a foundation for your life. In what do you place your ultimate trust?

❧ For further study read Luke 6:46-49.

❧

Lord, I confess my ignorance about building this house that You intend for me to be. I cry with the psalmist, "Who am I that we should be able to offer so willingly as this? For all things come from You." All this abundance with which we have prepared to build You a house for Your holy name is from Your hand and is all Your own. But unless You build my house, unless You are my foundation, my efforts are in vain.

O Lord, be my fortress, my rock, my foundation. There is no one but You. You alone have the words of eternal life; You alone are my strength. May I learn what it means to rest in You, to wait upon You as You build my house. In Jesus' name, amen.

❧

My Personal Reflections

_____

_____

_____

_____

_____

_____

_____

_____

_____

_____

_____

_____

_____

_____

_____

_____

_____

_____

_____

Two

❧

MEASURING UP

❧

"For I know the plans I have for you," declares the LORD, "plans to prosper you and not to harm you, plans to give you hope and a future."

— JEREMIAH 29:11 NIV

"There is almost a secret code among good builders," Bill told me. "I often saw my father inspect another builder's new home with a tape measure that he carried in his pocket, only to discover something out of whack. He would speak of this shortcoming with much disdain. A building out of square adds a great deal of work for the craftsmen who follow—for Sheetrock, siding, window, door, cabinet, and wallpaper installers. My father would say, 'This kind of sloppy practice adds headaches for everyone else who has to work on this house! It's better to measure twice so you only have to cut once.'"

After the foundation for our house was finished, Bill and his father began the important task of checking to be sure the building was both square and level. Bill told me that nothing was more frustrating in building than to have floors that tilt, walls that lean, and surfaces that do not take additional materials squarely.

Important as the foundation is, it's also essential that the building be accurately measured and made square and level from the very beginning so that the house will be true, upright, and fit together properly.

HONEY FOR THE HEART

How sweet are Your words to my taste,
Sweeter than honey to my mouth!

— PSALM 119:103

I wish I could say that with all of the Christian training I received in my home in my early years, I instinctively knew that I needed to measure my life against God's wisdom. But that didn't just happen. It is one thing to know certain things and quite another to *know* them, to follow them. We human beings resist being measured. Maybe it's because we know too well our own shortcomings. But over time, I have come to realize how important it is to submit my whole heart, my whole life to God's Word—that I needn't fear looking into the mirror of God's Word, but instead learn to love and desire the truth.

I have always loved books. I grew up in a home with no television, and our weekly library trips were highlights as my brothers and sisters and I could each get a stack of books for the week. The Bible, though, was a special book in our family. My father was a Gideon. Although I knew he was doing God's work, I was embarrassed one day to see him at my school, uncharacteristically dressed in his suit on a weekday, handing out copies of the New Testament to my fellow students.

At home when Dad reached for his big King James Bible before we went to school in the mornings, I would try to listen respectfully while I nibbled on a piece of toast or surreptitiously fussed with my hair. My mind was on what was going to happen in class that day or whether that cute boy would notice me. Dad didn't learn English until he went to grade school, and he quit school in the eighth grade to help support his family, so his reading was halting, tedious. He often read to us from the Psalms: "I will lift up mine eyes unto the hills, from whence cometh my help. My help cometh from the LORD, which made heaven and earth" (Ps. 121:1–2 KJV).

As I look back, I realize that certain images impressed upon me that the Bible was no ordinary book. When I was in the fifth grade, I had a teacher who read us a psalm every morning. One spring morning she read to us out in the play yard: "The heavens declare the glory of God . . . " And as I looked up into the vast Montana sky with clouds racing overhead, I knew I heard the truth. A few years later when I was a teenager at a youth camp, my counselor for the week read Ephesians to us in our afternoon devotions. I do not remember the counselor's name; I only remember that as I sat huddled on a top bunk bed in a rustic cabin, Ephesians came alive for me, because it was alive for her. She read the words carefully, slowly, her face glowing as if it were a love letter written exclusively to her. I suddenly saw the Bible as a personal, hands-on intimate communication.

But perhaps the most durable impression of the importance of God's Word is from my very early childhood. When I stumbled out into the kitchen in early mornings still full of sleep, I saw Mother at the kitchen table reading her Bible, coffee cup in hand. I always found a ready place in her lap until I was wide awake. The Scriptures captivated her, and she was always eager to share an insight she'd learned from poring over it. She got answers from that Book.

She never told me so directly, but I understood it years later as a young mother myself with small children. Our church had a morning Bible study that I enjoyed attending. But there were many Bible study mornings when I packed up the kids and threw a diaper bag over my shoulder only to discover that one of the children had a fever or an upset stomach. Then there were the times that I did get to the church only to find that the baby-sitter didn't, and what was the point of staying in the nursery?

It was after one such morning that I drove home from the church with tears of frustration. I believed God was interested in His children, but was He really interested in me? Me, with little ones and all that went with having small children—things such as allergies, ear infections, and a never-ending stream of laundry? Did He care about my secret longings and dreams? Where did I fit into His grand scheme? It occurred to me as I took my Bible out of the diaper bag that there was nothing stopping me from reading it on my own.

It is possible to have the Bible prominently displayed in your home and yet never let it be a real part of you. It was like that for me. The Bible was everywhere in my house—everywhere but inside me. Yes, I'd owned a Bible for years and read snatches of it here and there, but I'd never established a personal Bible study period.

So for the first time as a young mother, I simply started reading it consistently on my own, journaling what it seemed the passages were saying to me. This was the beginning of a fascinating adventure that has added an immeasurable depth to my life. I am not an educated scholar, and I have never been to seminary. I am simply an ordinary person who has found within the pages of the Bible a blueprint for life, a treasure available to you, too.

If you haven't already done so, start by getting your own Bible—a version you can understand—and begin reading a chapter or two at a time, taking care to reflect on what you read. Journaling your thoughts on what you're reading makes it personal, real. I also found it helpful to write on separate index cards specific verses that speak to me about certain issues in my life, referring to them often to help me memorize them, thus internalizing the truth.

A small-group Bible study can be very helpful, and there may be one through your church that you can become involved in. I highly recommend Kay Arthur's Precept Bible studies, available in Christian bookstores, and there are many other practical, useful tools as well to help you get into the Bible. But just do it—just start reading with an honest and open mind, asking as you read, "What does this passage, this story, say to me?"

I realize that not everyone has been exposed to the Bible, even in a society where it's readily available. And yet the principle is true: If we seek Him, we will find Him, because the Bible is simply truth for a hungry heart. Phillips Brooks, who pastored over a century ago, gave this timeless advice: "The Bible is like a telescope. If a man looks through his telescope, then he sees worlds beyond; but if he looks at his telescope, then he does not see anything but that. The Bible is a thing to be looked through, to see that which is beyond; but most people only look at it; and so they only see the dead letter."[1]

What a gift to have this amazing, universal, yet personal Book. It is more than a book. It is God-breathed. And through this treasure, He faithfully deals with us as we are, where we are. John White expressed it this way:

> God does not want to guide us magically. He wants us to know His mind. He wants us to grasp His very heart. We need to be soaked in the content of Scripture, so imbued with biblical outlooks and principles, so sensitive to the Spirit's prompting, that we will know instinctively the upright step to take in any circumstances small or great. Through the study of Scriptures, we may become acquainted with the ways and thoughts of God.[2]

THE BLUEPRINT

I am the LORD your God, who teaches you what is best for you, who directs you in the way you should go.

—ISAIAH 48:17 NIV

Living an upright life doesn't just happen; it takes adherence to a standard with greater integrity than we humans can manufacture. A big part of the measuring that goes into construction work is to see how the building matches up with the blueprint. One definition of blueprint is "a carefully designed plan." God's Word is the blueprint for our lives, and how essential it is to take time to study it, to reflect upon our lives to see if they fit the master blueprint. God does not intend for our lives to be haphazard, meaningless, but instead He has a carefully designed plan for us.

A builder I know goes to the lot, and after the foundation is poured, he walks around and visualizes the house. It's important to be thoughtful here. Look at the foundation, the subflooring. Now is the time to decide if you want to put two rooms in here or one big one. Measure . . . measure . . . look.

Proverbs 4:26 (KJV) says, "Ponder the path of thy feet, and let all thy ways be established." There are times to ponder our own paths, to be thoughtful about how we are building. We need times of solitude with the Word to ask ourselves some hard questions: What is the main thrust of my life? What am I doing that has eternal, lifelong consequences? What do I do about this anger or this deep well of hurt in my life? What about this anxiety that consumes me? What does God have to say about how I deal with it? How do I measure my life against the truth so that later I won't have to compensate for mistakes?

THE ONE AND ONLY EXAMPLE

> *Thus He showed me: Behold, the Lord stood on a wall made with a plumb line, with a plumb line in His hand. And the* LORD *said to me, "Amos, what do you see?" And I said, "A plumb line." Then the Lord said: "Behold, I am setting a plumb line in the midst of My people Israel."*
>
> —AMOS 7:7-8

Dale, a friend of ours, had an experience that vividly shows the importance of using the right standard in order to measure. When he was a teenager, he was helping his father build an art studio for his mother. His father gave him a piece of lumber cut to specific measurements. "Use this as a pattern, Dale, to cut this stack of lumber," he instructed.

But instead of using the original piece to measure the other boards, Dale used the second piece as the pattern for the third. He diligently cut all the boards, using each succeeding piece he cut as the pattern instead of the original one. He finished in record time and, pleased with his work, showed his father, who pointed out that the whole stack was cut wrong. Consequently, all of his work and material was wasted, and he had to start over.

A builder who ends up with a house with a crooked wall probably didn't start out with a board that was very crooked. The measurement was off just a bit—just a tiny bit. Still, it was off. This was illustrated pointedly to me when we were wallpapering a wall on a bathroom we'd added. In the process of wallpapering, we discovered that the walls were out of square, and trying to get the wallpaper on right over a crooked wall was a nightmare.

I don't believe anyone intends to live a corrupt life. I've never heard a young person say, "I want to become an embezzler when I grow up," or an alcoholic, or a gambler. It starts with a small compromise, taking the easy way rather than the right way. One has a brief thought, entertained a moment too long. I'm convinced that David, the man after God's heart, didn't mean to wreak such havoc in his family's life, nor in Bathsheba's life, nor in his kingdom. And yet that is what happened when he stood on his rooftop and gave a second look at Bathsheba. His life then began a downward spiral as he followed his own desires instead of what was right.

Life's blueprint is revealed in God's Word. It is our true plumb line, the perfect example. Human nature being what it is, we look for shortcuts. We want what's quick and easiest or what we can most readily see that looks good. What everybody else is doing or not doing subtly and slowly becomes the standard. It's tempting to think that if we have the world's approval or we impress the right people, then we've arrived.

William Booth, founder of the Salvation Army, went through a time of discouragement early in his ministry. Nothing seemed to be going well for him—his preaching wasn't right and he was criticized for his lack of education. His wife and coworker, Catherine, gave him this advice: "Never mind who frowns if God smiles."[3] And I would add: Never mind who approves if God doesn't. The Bible is full of stories of people who were encouraged to heed God's Word, to listen, to obey. The same principles apply to you and to me, too. Our Creator knows what is best for us even though at times we don't understand why.

SEEING THE REAL TRUTH

> *Let the word of Christ dwell in you richly.*
>   —COLOSSIANS 3:16

Truth is imparted to us in different ways, some of it distorted, which is why we must keep looking to God's Word, our original blueprint. I spent much of my childhood in church—a gift for which I'm grateful, although it took me a long time to understand what the true measure for my life should be. There are some things we must "unlearn," as well as things we must learn.

My home church is built like a rectangular box, with large windows of glass block which to this day make me feel claustrophobic. The entrance to my childhood church is a full flight of steep concrete stairs. Its very design and architecture speak to me of rigidity and impossible standards. In church we sang of grace but lived works— after all, "the night was coming," and there never was a finish line to work, especially in the spiritual realm. Always more wrongs to right, ways to be better, work harder, pray more. And the elusive prize—

acceptance—kept moving further and further out of reach. It is difficult to accept grace while one is earning it, and it has taken a lifetime for me to understand that the debt is paid, and I have nothing to do but accept grace.

Sometimes we look at another person and think, *If only my life could be like hers.* Or *If only I had the education and opportunity that he had.* Or, *If only my marriage partner was as spiritual as so-and-so, then I could live a good life.* Or, *If only my parents hadn't divorced. But look at my dysfunctional mess!* And then we try in some ways to emulate someone we admire, to be like him or her. While examples of others are helpful—and mentors are essential—they cannot be our pattern, our measure for our lives. No other human being can.

God's truth is the only perfect standard. Peace goes out the window the minute I measure myself against others, compare my life to someone else's life. As Paul wrote in 2 Corinthians 10:12, "But they, measuring themselves by themselves, and comparing themselves among themselves, are not wise." It isn't wise because God is building a unique dwelling place in each of us, and we must look to Jesus, the author and the finisher of our faith—the author and finisher of my spiritual house.

The measure that I wrongly used for much of my life was the acceptance of others. But good works, regardless of how exemplary, cannot sustain a life because I can never be good enough. None of us can. Paul said in Romans 3:23, "All have sinned and fall short of the glory of God." What I *do* is not enough, even though I thought I was doing much of it for God. It was only later, when I was forced to do a drastic remodeling of my life that I realized my "walls" were out of square. The subtle measure of "What will others think?" is not the plumb line that one should use to measure an enduring house for God.

The temptation to resist measuring with the truth is deeply ingrained. This was brought home to me just a few days ago. Our family was out of town on a little vacation, visiting relatives. We had planned to go to church with them, and I realized after we unpacked that I'd left our garment bag with its neatly pressed church clothes at home. Do we go to church in our casual clothes or not go to church at all? Our daughter Amy couldn't understand my dilemma. "Well, Mom, do you think God cares what you're wearing? The object is to worship." I told her it wasn't God's opinion I was worried about, and then it occurred to me that that was really the only opinion that mattered. We went to church just as we were.

As the sometimes archaic wrappings of my childhood faith slowly peel away, I am comforted—and, yes, surprised—to see beneath the man-made facade a gleaming solid-gold faith, tried in the fire and purified. Truth sometimes is hard, unyielding. But the real truth that stayed, covered with mercy, was the truth from God's Word implanted in me—the spirit of the law, not the letter of the law. That is what has stayed through the years, and that is what holds my life now, saying yes to an eternal, changeless God. "The grass withers, the flower fades, but the word of our God stands forever" (Isa. 40:8).

I thank God for the truth of His Word. It is a great comfort, security, and definition, but it also is a sword that continues to go to the quick of my life, a discerner of my thoughts and intents. Painfully sharp and true, like a surgeon's knife, truth can hurt; but it also sets me free. It makes me square up, level with myself and with God.

A WILLINGNESS TO BE MEASURED

> *"For my thoughts are not your thoughts, neither are your ways my ways,"*
> *declares the LORD. "As the heavens are higher than the earth, so are my*
> *ways higher than your ways, and my thoughts than your thoughts."*
>
> —ISAIAH 55:8-9 NIV

Perhaps the key to learning how to measure our lives against the truth of God's Word is seeing that only God can give us the best blueprint for our lives. It is easy to come to the Bible with a preconceived thought, a bias, looking for validation, but that kind of thinking is dangerous. I must come with an open mind to His Word, with a yieldedness and willingness to have my life corrected and cleansed.

I must come with an inner ear that is listening, knowing that only in Him is the right plan. Only by relying on His Word, making a personal study of it, and loving the truth can I build right.

Years ago Hugh Elmer Brown wrote:

> It is one thing to prowl through the Bible till one can steal a phrase with a catchy sound, around which, regardless of its original meaning, one may construct an essay, compose an oration, or rhapsodize a prose poem. It is quite another thing to deal honestly with the Scriptures, seeking to find in them a lantern for all feet, a blueprint for right living.[4]

Just last week while we were Christmas shopping in the city, our car was broken into, and my briefcase was stolen, among other things. Tucked inside my briefcase was the Bible Bill gave me on Easter nearly twenty years ago. We have several Bibles in our house, but this Bible was mine.

It's a loss difficult to articulate. The Bible was becoming worn, and I'd just remarked to Bill that it needed to be replaced, but I was reluctant to part with my old friend. Tucked within its pages were some of the current prayers I was praying for my family—specific needs with certain Scriptures that I was praying. Psalm 139 had as a marker in it a sonogram of Will, our first grandbaby. This Bible had been my blueprint for life in crucial times. There were passages marked in it that gave me assurance when we were adopting our daughter. I'd underlined verses in it as I sat in a darkened hospital room when Andy was in surgery. I had clung to its comfort during the deaths of my father and my mother. Each child had been prayed over, written in the margins. There were tearstains on the pages.

Glorious Scriptures that brought new insight and immeasurable joy were underlined, feasted upon, and starred. When I needed new wine in my marriage, Jesus' words and healing touch brought new life and understanding to me. Now in ever-changing midlife years, I would go to it every morning like a homing pigeon, gathering strength and wisdom for the day, simply learning how to be.

Yes, I feel the actual physical loss of my Bible. My son Eric gave me a new one for Christmas, and I have already marked in it, because it's my personal blueprint. But this loss, too, is in God's hands. Maybe it's time to step back and say, "Okay, God—take me further. Help me understand that the Bible is simply revealing You. Tell me more."

After all, when we measure in order to build, we do not exalt the tape measure or frame pictures of it on the wall or carry it around like a good luck charm. It's the function of the measure and the level that helps us build a good house. So it is not that we worship the ink and the paper. Loving God's Word is bigger than that. It's seeing past the letter of the law to the spirit of the law, to a personal God whom I can know. It's knowing there is a bigger plan for me and for you than our personal dreams and ambitions.

And we can only discover how to begin to build by making a lifetime study of His Word, by letting it become part of us, our lives. Internalizing it. Waiting on God. Not rushing ahead to do our thing, but waiting. Watching. Measuring against the Word—measuring against what we know is true—rechecking the blueprint to see if the dimensions we are constructing are right. Is this the right way to build? Is this the plan for us?

What is a builder without a plan, a tape measure, or a level? How could anyone put up walls that are straight and true without a plumb line to set the standard for the rest of the building? It would not be a viable house. And what is a Christian without a Bible? Without it, we are in a moral and spiritual vacuum with no point of reference.

Hundreds of years ago, Thomas à Kempis wrote, "It is a great thing to live in obedience, for we are too much ruled by our own passions."[5] We were not designed to be out of balance—to be "crooked" or tilted. And we know when we're not "right." Guilt and the conviction of the Holy Spirit reminds us there's something wrong. It's like an unbalanced scale—when one side is overloaded with sin (i.e., disobedience to God's Word), only repentance and obedience to God's Word brings our lives back into order.

There's a dramatic illustration in the book of Daniel (chapter 5) of the Lord bringing His Word to bear on a situation. God wrote a message to King Belshazzar on his walls in the midst of his elaborate feast. The prophet Daniel gave the king the chilling interpretation: "You have been weighed on the balances and have failed the test" (v. 27 NLT). Belshazzar was thoroughly corrupt, but how can anyone withstand the scrutiny of a righteous God? How can you; how can I? It is daunting, to say the least. There is only one true standard of righteousness and unrighteousness. Someday we will all stand before God, and His plumb line will be put to our lives. In that day will our names be in the Book of Life? Scripture says our works will be tried by fire, and they will either be burned up or remain. Will we hear His words, "Well done, good and faithful servant"?

It is only by throwing ourselves upon His truth as revealed in the Word—by accepting His holy covering—that we are able to stand. Above all, our God is merciful and faithful, and true to His nature. When we turn to Him, He is there. Walter Cavert wrote:

> It is one of the spiritual tragedies of our times that in taking the historical and literary dimensions of the Bible, we have neglected it as the book of life. We need now to spend less time in measuring the Bible, and more time in allowing the Bible to measure us. We need to submit our personal lives and our social conditions to the searching analysis of the prophets and of Jesus' teaching, to open our

minds and hearts to the Bible's flaming truths about justice and brotherhood, love and faith and moral power.[6]

WHAT ARE YOU USING
TO MEASURE YOUR LIFE?

❧ Consider for your own life the analogy of measuring. What guide or "blueprint" do you use to make decisions—small ones and large ones?

❧ How can you strengthen your "house for God" by learning to love and obey God's Word?

❧ Consider what you need to do to make God's Word a more integral, driving force in your life.

❧ For further study read Jeremiah 15:16; James 1:21-25.

❧

Lord, many voices call to us today, clamoring for our attention, begging to be heard and entertained. It is tempting to shape my life on what is convenient for me or makes me look good.

Help me to see and know the truth. Help me have a hunger to know Your Word so that I can hear Your still, small voice and, in doing so, know how I am to measure and plan my life. Lord, show me how to be. In Jesus' name, amen.

❧

My Personal Reflections

_____

_____

_____

_____

_____

Three

❧

HEARTWOOD

❧

Consider the quarry from which you were mined, the rock from which you were cut!

— ISAIAH 51:1 NLT

It was a late summer day when trucks brought the lumber for our house and stacked it next to the foundation. "I love this part of building," Bill told me, his eyes shining. "The wood. I love the smell, the feel of it, the actual material that's going to be our house."

There was a lot to learn about lumber. Some types of wood do not have structural integrity or the fiber necessary to hold a load without breaking. Heartwood—the core of the tree, the dense inner rings that give a tree backbone so that it can sway in the wind without breaking—is the sturdiest, and redwood and cedar are often used because they are most resistant to insects and decay. When a builder starts building a home, the usual code requires that lumber within six inches of the ground be heartwood. True heartwood is difficult to find these days. Recently I toured a pre-Revolutionary house in Charleston, South Carolina, that has on its original floors heart pine. It was beautiful tightly grained wood with no knots or imperfections.

"If you can't find heartwood," Bill went on to say, "you should use pressure-treated wood—wood condensed by a machine to make it 'tight-grained' like heartwood. This is the wood that we used next to the foundation upon which were placed the floor joists and wall framing. Heartwood or pressure-treated wood is extremely durable material to build with—it's sturdy stuff."

Childhood is like heartwood—the strong center close to the foundation of our lives, always there. We are undeniably products of our homes, our parents. Try as we might, we cannot escape it. Who I am is at the core of my being, just as heartwood is the core of the tree. How well do you know you? To fully appreciate the gift of your life, you must consider your own heartwood—the original material with which you began to build your life. And as you begin to understand it—the good and the difficult—you see that it is an integral, durable part of your house for God.

HEARTWOOD—A SPECIAL GIFT

> *Remember the days of old;*
> *Consider the years of many generations.*
> *Ask your father and he will show you;*
> *Your elders, and they will tell you.*
>
> — DEUTERONOMY 32:7

When we are children, we rarely comprehend the powerful material that we are given by our parents to help shape us into unique persons, depending upon our choices and direction. Perhaps it's just as well.

Not long ago on a sunny June afternoon, I stood among family and friends in a carefully tended cemetery in northern Montana. I broke off a pink carnation from the mass of flowers on top of the casket and cradled it in my hand. Each of us there that day came with his or her own set of memories to say good-bye to this woman. My mother had loved her family with a tenacious joy. Pride in who she was competed with anguish deep inside of me. It was unthinkable that she, too, was gone. A line of poetry came to me, somehow comforting in its defiance:

> *I am not resigned to the shutting away of loving hearts*
> *in the cold ground.*
> *I know, but I do not approve. And I am not resigned.*[1]

When we'd brought Dad here sixteen years ago, it was January and brilliantly cold, the air hurting our lungs as we breathed. It was near zero, the sky clear, the snow deep. I remember thinking, *A good day for a soul to go to God—so clear, no interference.* Other family members were buried here—uncles, a cousin, my grandmother next to my parents. After Dad's death, Mother had a headstone placed here, with her name and Dad's on it, with the inscription: "Till He Comes."

"Mother, how can you stand to see your name on that?" I'd asked her. It had seemed macabre to me, but she'd replied matter-of-factly, "Well, that's what Dad and I planned."

I came back to the present as I heard Bill read the final Scripture, the one Mother loved, "'Then we who are alive and remain shall be caught up together with them in the clouds to meet the Lord in the air. And thus we shall always be with the Lord'" (1 Thess. 4:17).

"We who remain." I looked around at my brothers and sisters, our growing-up children, our spouses, our extended family, and friends. *How fragile is this gift of life,* I thought. *How I've missed Dad, and now how keenly I will miss Mother. Even if I had not been her daughter, I'd want her for a friend and mentor.* She loved life and somehow never grew used to the sight of the sky. She'd say, "Oh, look!" with wonder in her voice, her brown eyes shining.

Like you, I had no choice in where I was born. My parents made their share of mistakes, but I was blessed to be a loved and wanted child. You may regard your "heartwood" differently. You may look upon your own childhood as something to forget, to just get over on your way through life. Regardless, the durable material that is your childhood is actually a gift to you, in its deprivation as well as in its blessings.

UNDERSTANDING YOUR GIFT

Self-knowledge puts us on our knees, and it is very necessary for love. For knowledge of God gives love, and knowledge of self gives humility.[2]

–MOTHER TERESA

My parents gave me a lasting gift, although on that day of farewell I didn't see it. But as time has passed, I realize that what they gave me—the raw material for my very life—is indeed far reaching. And so it is for all of us. This does not mean we are victims of circumstance; we choose our response to what we are given, the good and the bad. But the material bound up in childhood is a powerful gift, and forever we are grateful and resentful for it.

Late that night after Mother's funeral, the house was quiet, everyone worn out by emotion. Bill and I were in an upstairs bedroom of my childhood home, and after he was asleep, I lay awake, remembering. The black and white snapshots that filled my scrapbooks didn't do justice to my memories that were alive with color, passion, and dreams. Above all, hope.

My childhood home is now my brother Dan's place on what the locals call the North Bench part of Montana, where the description "Big Sky" originated. Out here you feel as if you're on the very crest of the earth. As lonely and isolated as it is, it seemed to me as a child that it was the top of the world. Off to the west rise the majestic

Rockies, and from the kitchen window, you can see the Sweet Grass Hills of Alberta to the north. The sky changes almost hourly as weather fronts from the west sweep down across the rolling prairies, now wheat and barley and cattle-ranching country.

Inside, I suppose I'll always feel like a Montana kid, and as long as I live, I will know it as my first home. In the springtime, I will wonder if the meadowlarks are singing. In the late summer, I will wonder how the harvest is. In the winter, I will wonder if there is enough snow for the winter wheat. Home is just inside of me, and no doubt it shows to the trained eye and ear.

I lay in bed, trying in vain to sleep. My heart felt full to the brim as I savored being "home" again, remembering what it had been like being tucked in bed safe in my parents' house, imagining them asleep in the bedroom downstairs. It seemed as if the past with all of its sights and sounds had swung around and dissolved into today, all a part of the now. I used to believe the past was behind me—that I progressed through time, much like being on a road with events and influences past. Now it seemed more like a circle—the past intertwining with the present—and here I am again.

I got up to open the window and knelt at the casement. It was a warm summer night, and the moon was bright outside, making shadows on the ground. I heard the same rustling of leaves in the same ash tree that I fell out of once, and there's a scar on my knee to prove it. The frogs in the pond past the barn filled the night air with their sound. The barn still stood, substantial, massive, in the moonlight. I'd spent hours there as a child. It always beckoned to me, holding out promises of fascinating things there—something to discover, some danger that seemed imminent. Accidents, rattlesnakes—you never knew what could get you, all the more reason for its attraction.

The barn was earthy, comfortable. Yet with its huge timbers and massive ceiling with doves in the rafters, it commanded a certain awe, not unlike an ancient cathedral. Built in 1876, it has stood the test of passing generations, holding their hopes and dreams, sheltering their animals, crops, and children. Now my nieces and nephews have the run of it.

But, of course, the past is past. My parents are gone; my brother Dan and his wife, Nancy, now own this family house that was built in 1910, and they are committed to farming this land. The rest of us children have scattered to different states and occupations. *How different we all are from each other,* I thought, *even with the same heritage, the same environment.* Yet our heartwood material is unique to each of us as we find our individual places in the world. Even within the same family, we are all uniquely gifted and wounded by the heartwood we are given.

A. W. Tozer wrote that "self-knowledge is so critically important to us in our pursuit of God and His righteousness that we lie under heavy obligation to do immediately whatever is necessary to remove the disguise and permit our real selves to be known."[3]

MY MOTHER AND FATHER

I have seen your face as though I had seen the face of God.

—GENESIS 33:10

As small children, we learn the basic imprint of God through our parents, and those images often follow us for a lifetime, often needing revision. I always thought my parents quite interesting, although my father was something of an enigma to me. There was no doubt in my mind that both he and Mother deeply loved God and the church.

For all Dad's apparent strength, somehow I knew even as a child that my father was a gentle soul that needed protecting. I would say, "Dad, tell me about your parents." "Well," he would respond with his

Swedish lilt, "there isn't much to tell." And that was all I could get out of him. Not until his death did I learn more about his early life from an aunt and a family friend. He took his crushing losses with silence and dignity, believing that to help someone less fortunate than he was the best solution for sorrow. "Into each life some rain must fall," he would say. A lot of rain fell into his early life, and in spite of his trying to forget it, it is my history as well.

He was known in the community for his kindness and generosity, serving for years on the school board, often reminding us children to be grateful we could be in school. We knew he was telling us of his disappointment in not getting to finish school, although true to his nature, he never would actually say that. His love for God, his family, and the land he found almost impossible to articulate. A curious combination, to have powerful, passionate emotions and not be able to express them. In fact, he couldn't tell us he loved us until he was dying.

Maybe the words were too terrifying, too powerful. Why tell people you love them only for them to leave you? Until he married my mother, that had been his experience: You love, you lose. The Pearson way of handling that was to work hard and be a good neighbor. Keep a stiff upper lip. I learned from him that I was to be good, make something of myself, be honest, and follow God.

As a young man, my father farmed north of Conrad with his brothers. He met my mother, appropriately enough, at the church in Great Falls where she lived and worked as a hairdresser.

What was my mother like, and how did her life affect mine? Somehow the first thing I want to tell you is that she was famous for her deep auburn hair. Perhaps it symbolized her personality, her passion for life, and her humor. A friend of Mother's once told me when I was very small, "Too bad you don't have beautiful red hair like your mother." I remember wondering what to say, a little wispy blonde-haired girl, drawing designs in the dust with my toe. "Um-hmm," I replied. I did take more after my father's side—the blond, stoic Swedes. I wanted to be more like my mother and her father and uncles who were in Vaudeville, but my serious heart knew instinctively that I wasn't.

Mother kept her hair long and, during the day, rolled up and pinned at the back of her head. At night she'd let down her hair and was transformed from president of the Women's Missionary Council into a flaming beauty. Dad loved her hair; every Christmas he bought her a dresser set—brushes, comb, and mirror. As she opened the gift, she would flash him her wonderful smile, and they exchanged looks. She always loved the gift and exclaimed over it. *How predictable,* I used to think. *Can't the man come up with something different, for crying out loud? A sweater, perfume, or something?*

When I was fifteen, Mother nearly died from kidney disease and had to remain in the hospital for three weeks. During her long stay, her hair became matted and dull, impossible to brush. One afternoon my older sister Janie and I, with Mother's urging, cut the red hair. She was relieved to finally be getting well, wanting to go home. Dad stood helplessly by as we cut off the long tresses while Mother made weak jokes.

After she got out of the hospital, she went to a beauty shop and got her hair styled and permed, which I thought made her look pretty and younger. She looked modern, like other moms, like Lucille Ball in *I Love Lucy.* And yet I missed her glamorous hair. The flamboyant, passionate woman that I knew lived inside of her came to the fore when at night she took out her pins, and her hair tumbled down her back.

Dad never bought her dresser sets anymore after that. For Christmas he got her things such as roasters and electric skillets.

HEARTWOOD CONTAINS
THE MOST POWERFUL MESSAGES

It takes some time to realize that it's the "unwritten rules" that are the strongest. These are just things you grow up knowing—for example, certain attitudes toward the opposite sex, money, ways to parent, or how you spend your time. We assimilate these "messages" from our earliest environment.

King David gave his son Solomon not only the materials to build the temple but also instructions. And according to Scripture, the finished product was breathtakingly impressive, unlike anything ever seen before.

Besides the actual physical materials, David gave his son influence . . . heritage . . . attitudes toward women, toward leadership. The good and the bad, all mixed up. He gave Solomon an example of a man with a heart after God, as well as a man with unbridled lust. Solomon made his own choices about what to do with that life-material. He built a magnificent kingdom; he was well known for his wisdom throughout the land, but his downfall was his alliances with pagan women.

Some of us were given very practical, helpful instructions in life; some of us were given damaging instructions. Some of us weren't given any instructions. Take some time to consider your own parents' written and unwritten "instructions" to you for life. It may take a while for you to see them. But along with the material and instructions we have a powerful gift—that of choice. It is up to us what we do with the instructions—whether we even hear them. That is why the "fear of the Lord is the beginning of wisdom," because that is where true wisdom lies. We listen; we watch; and then we prayerfully discern which messages we take in.

My father never gave me much verbal instruction on how to live my life. He just did not talk much. He simply set the parameters and seemed to assume I would find my way among them. If I were to try to imagine Dad's most important life-message to me, I think it would be: "Be steadfast, faithful. Don't be weary in well-doing, for in due season you'll reap, if you faint not." He also very clearly gave this message: "Avoid confrontation and controversy." He gave very clear yes-and-no responses to certain things in life, and when his mind was made up, it was made up; but he would not go out of his way to confront or straighten anyone out. There were times when I wanted him to "go to bat" for me or my siblings, but he would avoid the confrontation.

On the other hand, Mother would not back down from a confrontation, especially if it involved any of her children. She talked plenty; she elaborated, discussed, pondered, considered, provoked us to conversation. She also gave me a love for beauty and a sense of wonder at the world, a quizzical stance toward people, and an unshakable belief that the world was a wonderful place to be after all. Mother, above all, was fun. If I were to imagine her message to me, I could hear her say: "Give those closest to you your best—your family, your church, your community. Use your gifts for God, and you'll have a surprising, wonderful life."

Mother gave another unsaid message: "There are some things you should never talk about. And I won't say what they are!" Mother was a woman with a past, with a painful secret that took me years to discover. She died before I had the conversation with her that I wanted. When I'd begged her after I was married to fill in the unexplained blanks in her life, she only responded to me with few tearstained lines in a letter, telling me there were things that were just too painful for her to discuss. Not wanting to give her any pain, (like my father) I backed off. My sister Judy (like our mother) insisted upon the whole unvarnished truth, so some years later in a letter to Judy, Mother filled in the blanks. It was a story of love and betrayal and abandonment—but ultimately one of courage and redemption.

Now that I understand her life better, I love her more, not less. I only wish I could have told her so.

The heartwood material my parents gave me is interwoven in me, and, despite my denial, it comes up now and then like clover in my garden. From Dad I have a dogged sense of good works that, carried to extreme, becomes humorless, dry, and pushes me to burn-out. I am aware of my deeply ingrained bias that passion and spontaneity are suspect, not to be savored or enjoyed at peril of losing one's salvation (no dancin'!). I intensely dislike confrontation and avoid it whenever I can.

One of Mother's weaknesses (albeit an appealing one) was allowing spontaneity to rule. Reading the paper rather than fixing dinner, talking an hour or two with an old friend rather than making the kids mind. Looking at herself in the mirror and complaining about her looks, and lamenting over her arthritic hands that would not allow her to play the violin anymore. Mother was shy in the presence of certain people, and if she felt inferior to someone, she clammed up and became somebody I didn't know.

Sometimes I'm uncomfortably aware that here I am again, being like this. ("You are just like your mother!" "Just like your father!") I find myself in a familiar pattern with forces at work greater than what is obvious, all the while loudly proclaiming that I won't be that way; I won't make those mistakes with my children! And I see that my faults and frailties as well as my gifts are all mixed up in the whole package deal of who I am—all of it now mine—and, in turn, I pass on my own "heartwood" that undeniably affects my children's lives.

Early the next morning after the funeral, I pulled on my jeans and went outside, down the familiar graveled road past the farmhouse. I walked over to where the little country school had been, a place where I'd spent the first eight years of my education. It had been moved off its foundations and was now a Baptist church in a neighboring town. All that remained was a gaping open basement. I could still clearly see a shuffleboard triangle painted on the concrete. This impossibly small place that had once been a big part of my world was now deserted, overgrown with weeds. I looked into that hole and remembered one snowy winter afternoon having my feelings and knuckles bruised in a box hockey game . . . right there, by the wall. Memories flooded me. In this place we opened a window to the world and dreamed of new places. Here we memorized Tennyson, Sandburg, Whitman. We formed a strong sense of community. It was here I began to learn that I was an individual capable of doing more than I thought I could, and it was here that I was taught about a larger world and encouraged to dream of my place in it.

LEAVING HOME TO FIND IT

We must first see the vision in order to realize it; we must have the ideal, or we cannot approach it.

— LAURA INGALLS WILDER[4]

I walked around what was left of the little country schoolhouse and remembered how much I had wanted to leave home in my late teens. Home had seemed suffocating and confining to me then. I was hungry for life and eager to leave this place of Big Sky to see what was out there waiting to be discovered. It was the same feeling I'd had about the barn when I was a small girl—only it was the world that beckoned to me now. There seemed to be a path just for me, leading me to some destiny, some calling.

I thought of the day I left home for college in California in the fall of 1965. I was eager to go, but I was also beginning to understand the price of discovery. It meant leaving home, and home was in every fiber of my being—the farmhouse where I'd lived all my life, the trees behind the house where I would sit with a note pad and write, all my "secret places" where I could escape the noise of a large family and read and think.

And the price especially meant leaving people who were so much a part of me I couldn't imagine being without them—my dad and his gentle, steady blue eyes, a man of the soil; my mom, full of wisecracks and wisdom, sometimes driven by impulsive, funny ideas, or full of irritation as she tried to keep meals and laundry and kids straight. Always something to laugh with her about. My oldest sister Janie had already graduated from college and married. I was going to college with my older brother John, which made the parting easier. He was my hero, and I was convinced he was the smartest person on earth. I was leaving my younger brothers and sisters—Judy, Dan, Kitty, and Joe. We had never been separated before. How would I live without them, wake up mornings without them? I comforted myself by thinking I would be blazing the trail for them, scouting to see what was there, to see if it was safe.

The little gray Studebaker was packed. John was impatient to leave, this being his sophomore year. I had checked and rechecked all my earthly belongings—clothes mainly and a few treasured books. Where was Dad? I walked down past the barn to look for him. He was by a granary, fixing something. I remember crying as I walked, saying good-bye to the trees, the barns, the cat, Alfie the dog. The meadowlarks' song, the swallows wheeling in the air, the breathtaking enormous canopy of sky—how could I leave this for California, where towns all ran into each other so that you never even knew what town you were in? A place where you didn't dare talk to strangers? I only knew there was something inside me that said it was time to go—time to look for the Dream.

"Dad, we're leaving." I reached up to hug him and saw that he, too, was crying.

He stood, leaning on a shovel, clad in his usual overalls, sobs shaking his shoulders. Aghast at this emotional outburst from my father, I stopped crying. "Why, Dad . . ." He put his arms around me and gave me an awkward kiss, tears making rivers down his sunburned face, his Swedish blue eyes brimming. Oh, love can be a painful thing. I knew at that moment that he loved me, although he had never said so. To his thinking, there were some feelings, some emotions too big for words. And what you felt for your flesh and blood, one whose eyes mirrored yours—well, some things are impossible to say.

So you smile, wipe away the tears, and you say, "Call us soon, okay? Is there enough gas in the car? Have you checked the oil? Drive careful, you hear?" All the final exit statements that parents somehow have to say. What they want to say is, "Do you have to go so soon? Now wait . . . it seems there was something really important I was going to say to you, but for the life of me . . . What was it? Are you . . . really leaving, child of mine?"

Heartwood for My Children

About the time you begin to appreciate your own heartwood, you see your own children leaving, taking with them materials you have given them. Not long ago one of our sons, his eyes bright and a college degree fresh under his arm, left home to go live in the city to look for work. And what was I doing? Fussing in the kitchen and laundry room, putting things together for him, finding towels and sheets and mismatched things for the kitchen. A couple of bags of groceries. Mundane, busy work to occupy my mind so I wouldn't have to see what was really happening. This, too, is part of parenting, giving things to my children as they leave to make a home, giving them nourishment for their journey. Unconscious at the moment that what we parents have already given them—the heartwood of their lives—will nourish and challenge them always.

In *In Search of Stones*, Scott Peck writes about his growing-up children:

> Now they don't want our caring. That is to say, they do and they don't. They want our admiration and gifts and money, but they don't want us. They don't want any of our wisdom. Certainly they don't want any of our advice. They also don't want to hear our stories. Partly that may be because they suspect some word of advice to be hidden in our stories even when it isn't. And partly it's because they're simply not interested. They have their own lives to live. They do want us to be interested in their lives, as long as there's no hint of desire to help, much less control. But at this point they really couldn't care less about our lives. In a sense, they want us to like them but not to love them anymore. And sometimes, even though they're our own children, it's not so easy for us to like them when they're so different from us, when they no longer want our concern, and when their desire for our liking is so much of a one-way street.... It is our task as parents, at least when our children are young, to stand beside them: to brood over them, to walk beside them so as to protect them from harm whenever possible.
>
> But we cannot be them. We cannot be inside their souls. They are foreigners to us. No matter that they issue forth from our loins, no matter how many years we walk beside them, guarding them, we are inevitably outside them. They are separate. Lonely though it might be for both them and us, as parents, we are outsiders in relation to our children.[5]

It is as though we are compelled to give our children things as they leave, along with words of advice. Perhaps this is what David was doing for Solomon, giving him the material and the instructions to build the temple: "Here. You build it. I've done the best I can— you carry on." My father's work-worn hands saw to it that we were clothed, fed, and on our way to college—a dream he'd never been able to afford. It was as if he were the stage—he lay down and let us dance on him, and we played on, unaware of his own dreams that died so that ours may live.

I never was able to thank him for that, for loving me that much. There were times I resented his stoicism, his dogged sense of duty, that he had never been much "fun," never hugged me and told me he loved me. But he showed me the only way he knew how, and now that I have watched my four sons drive away, their father and I waving from the driveway, I am more forgiving. It is hard to let our children go. It is hard to leave our parents, for some of us harder than for others. It is hard to separate; yet we must.

Why is this memory of leaving home to this day so real, so vivid in my mind? Perhaps it was due to the dramatic contrast between the cultures of rural Montana and southern California in the sixties. But it was more than that. It was a birth into the world that would take me on a path never to return home, except for brief visits, for reunions, for an occasional harvesttime. And to bury my dead.

I can't remember what my mother was doing the day I left. There was always plenty to do in the kitchen—meals that still needed fixing, younger children to corral. I only remember that my father—the man who never cried—wept.

I thought I left home. What I didn't know was that the heartwood of my life would forever be with me, influencing me in ways I couldn't have understood then.

> To depart is to die a little. But to stay is to die a little, too. One must have a place before one can give it up. One must receive before giving, exist before abandoning oneself in faith. We receive a place only so as eventually to leave it, treasure only so as to cast it away, a personal existence only so as to be able to offer it up.[6]
>
> —PAUL TOURNIER

DO YOU REMEMBER?

❧ leaving home for the first time?

❧ getting homesick?

❧ coming home again, after first leaving?

❧ your father's and/or mother's written and unwritten "instructions" to you? How have they influenced your life?

❧ What are you contributing to the heartwood of your own children?

❧ For further study read 1 Chronicles 17; 29; 2 Chronicles 1-7.

❧

Lord, thank You for all the events that have shaped me so far. You have given me a powerful, wondrous gift, and I thank You for the heartwood of my life. There are parts of it that I would rather not have; and yet I see that so often the best gifts are not the ones I wanted—but they are the ones I needed. Thank You. Help me to be grateful for what I have been given and to allow You to form it into something beautiful and useful.

I pray that together You and I will craft from the raw material of my life a "house for God," a place where You are at home and where others are loved. In Christ's name, amen.

❧

My Personal Reflections

_____

_____

_____

_____

_____

_____

Four

❧

FRAMING

❧

I set before you today life and prosperity, death and destruction. For I command you today to love the LORD your God, to walk in his ways, and to keep his commands, decrees and laws. . . . Now choose life, so that you and your children may live and that you may love the LORD your God, listen to his voice, and hold fast to him, for the LORD is your life.

— DEUTERONOMY 30:15-16, 19-20 NIV

It seemed that it took forever to finally get the actual building of our house underway. Bill and his father had carefully gone over the plans; they saw the foundation poured, being certain that it was square and level; the subflooring was in place, the lumber ordered and delivered. And then one day I drove to the building site with the children, and we were amazed to see—overnight it seemed—our house actually up. It stretched three stories tall, and as the boys stood in their roughed-out bedroom, they were able to touch the lowest branch of the giant Ponderosa tree. It was becoming real. We really were going to have a house.

"This is an exciting time of building," Bill told me, "the pitchy smell of the freshly sawn wood, the studs and walls going up against the sky, the house now suddenly looming large. The short time it takes to frame a house always surprises me. Of course, it's only a skeleton, but you can see the definite shape of the house."

Just as framing shapes a house, and a skeleton is the shape of a human body, certain important choices shape your life and my life. The framing years, driven by passion and maybe a little bit of insanity, seem to go fast. It seems that it's in the young adult years where we make life-shaping choices, often at an accelerated rate—where to attend higher education (if at all), what work to pursue, whom to marry (if one marries), how many children to have, and where to live. These are important, life-shaping choices.

But there are choices we make that are much more subtle and yet just as influential. They are the decisions of the spirit and of the will that ultimately shape our lives, our belief systems that form our character throughout life. Or, if we choose wrongly, they can cause our lives to collapse upon us.

CHOICES THAT FRAME OUR LIVES

The greatest gift that God in His bounty made in creation and the most comformable to His goodness and that which He prizes the most, was the freedom of the will.[1]

— DANTE

One builder reminded me that although it's tempting during the framing process to hurry, this is a good time to be thoughtful, deliberate. "It is a creative place to be," he said. "As the framing goes up, you now have a chance to see the view, to feel what the house will be like." Perhaps a window needs to be bigger, or the door can be set in a different place. Here is an opportunity to make significant structural modifications inside the rooms, to refine their shape. After all, the design should reflect you. The idea of building your own home is to have one supportive of you and your family. It should be a comfortable, authentic house that gives you a place from which to grow and confidently face the world.

And so it is that you and I have the precious gift of the human will to shape our lives by our choices. We are not always aware of this gift, and at times we are reactors to life rather than responders. One of the most profound stories I have read on the human will is a small book, *Man's Search for Meaning*, the personal reflections of Viktor Frankl.[2] He wrote out of his traumatic experiences in the Nazi death camps. His message is that we always have a choice regarding our response to whatever life gives us, regardless of the circumstances.

Last Christmas as I made my list for my husband and children, I pondered what to get them. I wanted them to have the best gifts ever. But it occurred to me that the gifts I really longed for them to have were not something I could buy and wrap up. It would be confidence for one child, discipline to exercise for another, involvement in a good church for one son. Certainly I could encourage or make suggestions. But it is their will that will build (or tear down) their own lives. As I was in the frenetic pace that can come at Christmas, a further question came to me: So what's the real gift that *you* need? It took me several days to realize that it was peace I needed. And for me to add this dimension to my life, I needed to exercise my will to receive peace—by trusting in God, by having faith, by praising Him even when I didn't feel like it. Even God will not usurp our will. He offers each of us precious gifts, but we must determine to receive them.

This is perhaps the most important aspect of framing our lives—simply to be aware of this incredibly powerful gift of choice. Often when we are young, we don't make conscious choices. Instead we choose on the basis of what is most convenient, what makes us feel secure or comfortable at the time, what has the most appeal. This is natural. My daughter, who is a sophomore in high school, recently was trying to decide if she should go out for volleyball. I suggested she take a blank sheet of paper, draw a line down the middle of it, and list the pros and cons. Her reasons listed for not going out were many and compelling: She could work harder on her homework; she could be free on weekends to do family things; she could work at a part-time job and earn some money; she wouldn't have to travel to games and get home so late. She only had one reason listed on the pro side: "Friends." Guess what? She went out for volleyball.

THE FRAME OF FAITH

> *The only thing I can give to God is "my right to myself." If I will give God that, He will make a holy experiment out of me, and God's experiments always succeed.*[3]

> —OSWALD CHAMBERS

The most important choice anyone could ever make is the decision to frame our lives upon the One True Foundation, using the plumb line of the Word of God. As I entered my teens, I became aware of my responsibility for my own soul. I wanted my own way. I wanted to taste all that life had to offer, whether or not it fit my foundation.

One quiet evening at an altar in a small chapel on my college campus during my freshman year, God and I had a confrontation. It meant accepting grace from God that He would receive me as I was, where I was. Although I'd grown up with a "foundational truth," at that point in my life—because of my own thought processes—I needed to reaffirm that choice as a young adult. Richard Foster writes, "The needed change within us is God's work, not ours. The demand is for an inside job, and only God can work from the inside. We cannot attain or earn this righteousness of the kingdom of God; it is a grace that is given."[4]

I have found that a yes to God is a cornerstone yes. It is a simple yes, but it holds power. When I was young, I said yes to God's grace and redemption. Now I was faced with saying yes to His will, His structure for my life. Saying yes to God is not a one-time thing. If our choices, our framing, is to be of His design, continual yeses will be required. To give one's will to one's Creator is a wondrous gift—one that He delights in. Hannah Whitall Smith prayed, "Lord, I am yours; I do yield myself up entirely to You, and I believe that You do take me. I leave myself with You. Work in me all the good pleasure of Your will, and I will only lie still in Your hands and trust You."[5]

Dr. Helen Roseveare, who experienced terrifying persecution as a missionary doctor during the Congo uprising in the 1960s, recounts that for her, choosing to place her life completely in God's hands meant accepting the cup of suffering without needing to fully understand why.[6]

Making Jesus Lord of your life when you are making critical choices is essential to framing a house for God. He cannot be an afterthought or an incidental part of the process. What does it mean to frame your life with this in mind?

I believe it means to seek His will in the other important life-shaping decisions. I believe it means to be prayerful in our decisions, wanting to live our lives to please Him. This is not as simple as it sounds because, of course, our own ambitions and dreams can become all mixed up in the equation. It is a process of weighing decisions, asking, "Will this build my life for eternity? Will this choice take me closer to God? Or is it contrary to what it means to build for eternity?" When we're young, and life is fresh and new, and opportunities seem abundant, it can be tempting to make the choices that seem the most lucrative, that appear to be the best for my success.

THE FRAME OF MARRIAGE

> *Come live with me, and be my love,*
> *And we will all the pleasures prove,*
> *That valleys, groves, hills and fields,*
> *Woods or steepy mountain yields.*[7]

While I was at college, it seemed that suddenly my life was taking shape, and choosing to become engaged to Bill, a graduate student, was a big step. Bill and I were in love, and we wanted very much to be together. We had common goals of service to God and thought we would make a good team. It seemed only logical to marry.

During the warm Montana summer I was engaged to Bill, I worked at a small diner in the middle of Conrad run by a woman named Minnie Ethel. Her claim to fame in town was her banana cream pie that she made from scratch (daily, so it would be fresh). In the afternoons Lillian and Mildred, who worked across the street at J. C. Penney's, would come over for pie and coffee. They had known my parents before I was born, and they couldn't get over the fact that I was throwing my life away on this Bill guy from California. Anybody from California was suspect, but especially somebody who drove a snazzy red car and planned to be a preacher. That was my Bill.

One day Lillian turned to Mildred as she finished off her pie and said in front of me, "Someday she's going to wonder why she was in such an all-fired hurry." Mildred agreed, and I seethed inside, *What do those old women know of love?*

George Bernard Shaw wrote, "When two people are under the influence of the most violent, most insane, most illusive and most transient of passions, they are required to swear that they will remain in that excited, abnormal and exhausting condition until death do them part."[8]

So it was that on August 20, 1966, at 8:20 P.M. (so the harvesters could get to the wedding), Bill and I pledged our lives to each other forever on this earth. We drove away toward San Francisco for our first jobs as youth pastor and church secretary with scarcely a backward glance. Leaving home this time was different, less wrenching. This time when I left home, I was leaving to establish a new home with my husband.

It is taking me a lifetime to understand this significant choice to marry, to appreciate God's gift of covenant marriage with all its beauty and difficulty. As in the choice to follow God, it is a decision that requires reaffirmation as one grows through life. It is a choice that must be bathed with forgiveness and purified in the fire of ordinary life. There is much to learn in this choice about trust and caring. Trust between a man and a woman is a delicate and fragile quality. We are so different from one another after all, and to understand and trust one another takes much listening. It is a complicated choice with profound implications.

THE FRAME OF FAMILY

Jonathan William was born one rainy November day in 1968. Bill said to me that day as we cradled our baby son, "Our lives are absolutely perfect. I love you; I love my son; I love where we live; I love what I do." We thought, *This is complete happiness, what we've always wanted. Look what we've made—a beautiful little son!*

In the next eight years, we added three more sons to our family—Eric, Christian, and Andrew, and we moved to Oregon. When Andrew was eight years old, we adopted our daughter Amy from Korea. By this time we lived below the beautiful Three Sisters mountains in the Oregon Cascades. Each child added a new dimension to our family structure, to my life. As I look back on those gathering, framing years, they were frenetic, but they were fun, as I found myself consumed by family.

The early 1970s was a difficult—although exhilarating—era to be a woman. When I was just beginning to have my children, there was a lot of women's liberation talk. I was a prime candidate to listen, because I'd married early, putting a husband and family first in my life. And I had dreams of my own that I had tucked so far back on a shelf I'd forgotten what they were, except in quiet moments. The unspoken question would surface: *What about me?*

A couple of months after our beautiful Andrew was born, I was standing at the kitchen sink. Bill was traveling with a mission organization, and I felt isolated, lonely, and bored. It seemed to me real life was happening somewhere out there, and here I was—sidelined. I prayed, "God, I need something that really challenges me, something I can sink my teeth into!" Right at that moment three-year-old Christian tugged at the back of my skirt and asked, "Mom, will you play this game with me?" Here was my answer: *These children are your calling.*

I sat down and played that game with Chris, knowing God had spoken. Caring for a child may be one of the purest ministries, although it certainly isn't glamorous, and is one of the most difficult in the world. In John 13 Jesus, "knowing who He was," picked up the towel and washed the disciples' feet. Caring for little ones takes incredible strength and sacrifice. No one sees you; your children greedily take your offerings of love and service for granted (as we did from our parents), assuming it is their right. Saint Teresa of Avila wrote in the 1500s, "Proof of spiritual love is that you strive in your household duties to relieve others. You also rejoice and praise the Lord in this way. All these things, not to mention the great good that they provide in themselves, will also help very much to further peace and unity."[9]

I found that in spite of myself, the Lord was very near to me then. Perhaps it was because He is accessible to us in the common things of our lives. The cup of water. The breaking of bread. In welcoming children into our arms. In fellowship over a meal, of giving thanks. A simple attitude of caring, of listening. Of lovingly telling the truth.

It is still a challenge to be a woman, to juggle all the choices. Maybe it's even more difficult now because there is pressure to be educated, successful, good-looking, and to produce wonderful families besides. And when you are a Christian, there is an added dimension—to be a godly woman, to bring up your children in a world hostile to righteousness.

Now I see my nieces, my daughter-in-law consumed by this framework of "family," of trying to make it all work. What I want to tell them most is yes, they have made important choices that frame their lives, but there are other, more subtle framing choices that truly are life-shaping. They are "heart-choices."

HEART-CHOICES
THAT FRAME A LIFE

If we could see beneath the surface of many a life, we would see that thousands of people within the Church are suffering spiritually from "arrested development"; they never reach spiritual maturity; they never do all the good they were intended to do; and this is due to the fact that at some point in their lives they refused to go further; some act of self-sacrifice was required of them, and they felt they could not and would not make it; some habits had to be given up, some personal relation altered and renounced, and they refused to take the one step which would have opened up for them a new and vital development.[10]

— OLIVE WYON

Choosing to Grow

Let us pursue the knowledge of the LORD. His going forth is established as the morning; He will come to us like the rain, like the latter and former rain to the earth.

— HOSEA 6:3

I had just fed Eric, who was a few months old at the time, and I was busy trying to clean up when suddenly I stopped, overwhelmed by the thought that I was a mother of two now, a wife of a minister. How had I gotten here? It was so unlike what I thought it would be, to be grown up and married. I remembered Mildred's comment to Lillian, and I reluctantly acknowledged there had been times when I wondered what my all-fired hurry was to be married. I had to confess that at that stage of "framing" in my life, I hadn't been deliberate or thoughtful. I'd been passionate and impulsive. It had seemed somehow in the blush of fresh love that marriage, ministry, and raising a family was all set to grand, glorious background music. It wasn't. And while I wasn't sorry I married early, I was learning that family life was incredibly hard. A crucible. I did not know I was such a selfish person, but marriage and motherhood was fast revealing it to me.

And where did I go from here? It was what I had always wanted when I was growing up, I thought—to build a life of significance, of service. But I knew life was requiring something more of me; indeed, there seemed to be much ahead, much that I did not know and was not equipped to handle.

It was a moment of epiphany. I stopped midair in what I was doing and made a promise right there in my kitchen: "Whatever happens in my life, I promise that I will keep growing—that I will never stop learning as long as I live." I said it simply, almost as a prayer, but I have never forgotten that moment. I remember setting an empty bottle on the countertop as I said it, the moment forever fixed in my mind. I did not fully understand that moment, but I knew I needed to frame my life with a choice to grow, to learn.

I thought then that the obstacles I had to overcome to have a successful life would be "finances" or "opportunity." What I did not see then was that the real obstacles to growth were not as obvious but every bit as intimidating. They are the things that lie inside of me—my negative attitude, self-centeredness, pride, low self-esteem. But I know now that as I chose to grow, each challenge became like another piece of wall, another room added to my life, making it bigger, more productive. Growth inevitably involves risk. The steps of growth come at the moments I would most like to avoid—often the places of my weakness and fears, but these offer a place to grow a larger, bigger life. One with more responsibility perhaps, but more wonderful. The learning never stops—and with learning comes new choices.

But this greediness to learn, to grow bigger, must be tempered by submitting our will to the will of God, or it can be a dangerous choice, taking me to harmful things. After all, the heart is deceitful and desperately wicked. The heart can betray me if it is not submitted to God.

My artist friend Kathy tells me that a significant choice she has made is to study art and literature. She learned this from her parents, who early in their marriage made similar choices; for instance, they chose to buy fine art rather than furniture, to invest in a valuable leather-bound set of Shakespeare instead of a new kitchen appliance. They chose to travel to wonderful, exotic places, to accept opportunity in unusual places instead of job security. While some may find this a risky choice, with the discipline of the foundational belief in God and measured with the Word, this choice has influenced Kathy to frame her life to see beauty and meaning in the world around her and to create thoughtful, provocative art.

Build thee more stately mansions,
O my soul, as the swift seasons roll!
Leave thy low-vaulted past!
Let each new temple, nobler than the last,
shut thee from heaven with a dome more vast,
Till thou at length art free,
leaving thine outgrown shell by life's unresting sea![11]

—OLIVER WENDELL HOLMES

Choosing to Trust

Trust in the LORD with all your heart, And lean not on your own
understanding; In all your ways acknowledge Him, And He shall
direct your paths.

—PROVERBS 3:5-6

This is one of the most important framing choices we ever make in life, although it's extremely subtle, and many of us never think about it. It is an attitude we adopt: Do I have a sense of trust toward God (which ultimately affects my attitude toward others)? Or am I convinced deep down that He is "out to get me"? Perhaps more common, some of us have internalized a deep-seated belief that if anything is going to get done, we must do it. This colors our attitude toward our family, toward our spouse, and toward our close associates.

Of course, we know that all people fail and that it is only God's grace in others that we can trust. And yet when we wholeheartedly trust God, we are able to let go of the need to control, and we can more readily accept people at face value. Oswald Chambers wrote, "I surrender myself—not because it is bad; self is the best thing I have got, and I give it to God; then self-realization is lost in God-realization. There is a subtle form of pride which is set on my holiness; in sanctification there is no pride."[12]

Learning to trust is a place of growth for me right now in the framework of my life. I realize I haven't fully trusted God with some things closest to me. As a consequence, worry, anxiety, and the need to control pop up in the most unexpected times and places. Trust is bringing a much-needed dimension to my life, and I'm learning that it requires a constant letting go—letting go so I can "grab on" to trust in God's goodness and provision. The psalmist wrote, "In God I have put my trust; I will not fear" (56:4). And trust brings peace— a precious commodity.

Choosing to Dream

"You have dwelt long enough at this mountain. Turn, and take your journey. . . ." "Look, the LORD your God has set the land before you; go up and possess it. . . . Do not fear or be discouraged."

— DEUTERONOMY 1:6-7, 21

Perhaps our greatest hindrance in framing a large house for God is that we do not wholly trust, wholly believe that God gives us certain gifts. Maybe the tendency to play it safe comes out of fear. There's nothing wrong with small houses—they can be beautiful and efficient, too, but they can also be limited. We must be sure we are building a house big enough for the dreams God can birth in us.

When we were in the process of moving seventeen years ago, I found a box of journals and diaries that I had kept all through my school years, fueling my passion to write. I'd even sold my first short story when I was sixteen years old, but life got too busy to write. My dream got shelved for a while, except for the wistful longing that reminded me there was an abandoned dream in the corner of my soul that needed attention.

Then late one evening while sorting through boxes, I unexpectedly discovered the journals in the garage, and I hugged them to myself like long-lost children, crying. "Where have you been? I've missed you so!" It was like finding my self again. I had sometimes felt that my soul had oozed through my fingertips into the diaper pail or dishwater. But here was concrete evidence that I had a self. I began journaling again, as I sat up late nights waiting up for a load of jeans to dry. I began jotting down an early morning thought with coffee and devotions.

As I look back over the early framing years, I was very attracted to seminars at that time—practical how-to seminars—how to raise children, the Basic Youth Conflicts, the self-improvement seminars. I needed material that made my life work: "Give me an outline and ten easy steps, please. And hurry." One can't afford to be terribly introspective and deep when one is at this hectic place in life! Yet . . . "deep calls unto deep," and in His time our lives become beautiful.

James Allen wrote:

> Cherish your visions; cherish your ideals; cherish the music that stirs in your heart, the beauty that forms in your mind, the loveliness that drapes your purest thoughts, for out of them will grow all delightful conditions. "Ask and you shall receive." Dream lofty dreams, and as you dream, so shall you become. The greatest achievement was at first and for a time a dream. The oak sleeps in the acorn; the bird waits in the egg; and in the highest vision of the soul a waking angel stirs. Dreams are the seedlings of realities.[13]

I look back at pivotal points in my life when I thought I was making the most critical choices. Such as, "I'll choose this college because it's close to the beach and my brother goes there." And because I went there, I met the person I fell in love with, and I pledged to spend the rest of my life with him. And then our children ended up going to that college and making lifetime friends, finding mates. Sometimes I stop and say, "God, are we framing my life together? Or is my life just sort of happening?"

Twenty-five years after Bill and I left college, we were back on campus, the speakers for chapel that day, with two of our sons as students there. As I look back, I see how those early choices of marriage and children radically shaped my life. Sometimes I wonder, *What if I'd done this differently? How would my life be now?* Back then I had no idea what was ahead. I was grabbing the hand of a wonderful man, eagerly pursuing marriage and family, and I had no idea how hard it would be. I also had no idea how wonderful it would be—sharing hopes and dreams—the incomparable thrill of having children, the warmth of knowing my husband's committed love.

Overwhelmingly, I am grateful for my life, in all its complexities and challenges. However, I am especially grateful for choosing to grow within my circumstances, choosing to trust, choosing to dream. And, most important, I'm grateful for a chapel on this campus where one lonely night with no one else in the room, I said yes to His will. I am so glad for that. It was the best choice of my life.

> We search for a self to be. We search for other selves to love. We search for work to do. And since even when to one degree or another we find these things, we find also that there is still something crucial missing which we have not found; we search for that unfound thing too, even though we do not know its name or where it is to be found or even if it is to be found at all.[14]
>
> —FREDERICK BUECHNER

LOOKING AT YOUR FRAME

❧ What are the significant choices you are making, and how have they shaped your life?

❧ What subtle, less-obvious choices can you now make to enlarge your life?

❧ For further study read Acts 9 through 11.

❧

Lord, I want to say yes to You with my whole heart, my whole life. But to follow You can be frightening. You said to the rich young ruler, "One thing you lack." That one thing was next to his heart. So many of my choices have been self-serving and shortsighted.

But I thank You that You are merciful and faithful, that You lead me step by step, and You never fail to meet me with open arms whenever I turn toward You. Teach me what it means to build more stately castles in my soul—a place for You to be at home with me—a place where You are honored by my life. In Jesus' name, amen.

❧

My Personal Reflections

_____

_____

_____

_____

_____

_____

_____

_____

_____

_____

Five

THE BEARING WALL

❧

O LORD our God . . . I know . . . that You test the heart and have pleasure in uprightness.

—1 CHRONICLES 29:16-17

Why do some houses survive with grace and beauty while others do not? At the very outset, a house must be built defensively. Bearing walls are essential to the sturdiness of a house. "Where is the bearing wall in this room?" I asked Bill as we stood in the living room.

"Here." He pointed to the shortest wall in the living room—the one with the most windows. "Actually, all outside walls must be bearing walls," Bill went on to say. "They are cross-braced and strongly reinforced. This wall can take the pressure. It holds up the twenty-five feet of ceiling that slopes down from the loft around the fireplace and the rest of the house."

As I walked through my house, newly appreciative of bearing walls, I thought how we—the house's inhabitants—blissfully go about the business of living, taking for granted our sturdy, speechless walls.

TESTING THE FRAME

If you do not bring any strain to bear upon timber, one kind is as good as another. A splinter of a broom is as good as the best ash or hickory

if you do not put any weight upon it. . . . And when men are tried in
life, what they are is made to appear.[1]

— PHILLIPS BROOKS

The bearing wall speaks to me of testing my commitment to truth, my
obedience. It is deliberate, responsible work to build an enduring
house for God, and the issues are not always clear. It's always easier to
go the way of least resistance. But the bearing wall, truth, reminds me
to live with intent, with a single purpose. Jesus said, "A divided household falls" (Luke 11:17 RSV). It is at the important points of my
"framework"—my significant choices—where I feel pressure most.

Can My Truth Survive Testing?

The year I was sixteen, the world began to open to me in wonderful
ways. But at the same time, I was becoming aware of the ugly, confusing side of life. I'd learned with growing horror of the Holocaust.
The Civil Rights movement was in full swing, making me aware of
the inbred injustice in my own country. And worst of all, Vietnam's
tragedy reached our community as a neighbor's son was killed there.
The God I had seemed to love and pledged to serve with all my heart
as a child seemed far removed. Inwardly I questioned, *Why should I*
believe in God just because this is what I've been taught? Who says I
need God? Or that this is the "god" I need?

One night after supper, Mother and I were doing the dishes, a
time when we had our best talks. As she washed and I dried, we
could say important things and be spared the scrutiny of a face-to-
face talk. The debate raging inside me was reaching a boiling point,
and I felt I'd die if I couldn't unburden myself. Mother was my safest
choice, but I wasn't certain of her reaction. I'll never forget that
moment as, heart pounding, I opened my mouth. "Mom," I blurted,

tears welling in my eyes, "I've been thinking. I don't believe there is a God. It all seems like a cruel joke."

Mother wiped her hands on a dish towel and laughed a little as she pushed a strand of auburn hair back from her face. She looked at me, her brown eyes gentle: "Of course God is there, Nancie. And it's okay that you're thinking. What good is anything if you can't question it?" Her eyes were intent with amusement, tenderness, pride. "He'll always be there for you," she said confidently. "Now let's get these dishes done."

Later I wondered, *Why didn't she tell me I was going to hell? Why didn't she wring her hands at the thought of her daughter rejecting the faith? What made her so sure there is a God?* The fact that she laughed completely disarmed me and somehow brought immeasurable relief. I didn't fully understand why; I only knew that later in life, her response to me then was pivotal—a moment of testing God's mercies, and they held.

Enemies of the Truth

Our major commitments give our lives definition, shape, and it is often at these places where we face testing. But a commitment isn't really a commitment until it's tested. Otherwise, what is it? Words on paper, an empty pledge. The "bearing wall" of commitment to God's truth reinforces my life, and of course this most critical framework of my life will be tested. We should not be surprised at this, yet often we are defeated by the sheer difficulty of doing the right thing.

Besides being drawn away by our own human needs and wants, we must open our eyes to the fact that there is an enemy of our souls. This fact has been graphically illustrated to me by my work in the women's prison. As I have talked to the women in prison over the past seventeen years and heard their stories, the scars of sin and

Satan's influence is clearly visible in their lives. Scripture refers to him as our "adversary." He doesn't want us to succeed spiritually. We on the outside mask our insecurities better than women in prison, and in our comfortable American lifestyle, we can operate under the illusion that there is no devil, no evil. But sooner or later, if we take a stand to do what is right, our resolve will be tested by the enemy.

Many voices in our world speak directly against what we know is right. We are bombarded on all fronts by our culture with the message that we are to gratify self, fulfill self. But followers of Christ can welcome testing, rather than be afraid of it. Goethe wrote, "The absence of temptation is the absence of virtue."

Where You Stand Is Holy Ground

The battle is lost or won in the secret places of the will before God, never first in the external world. The Spirit of God apprehends me, and I am obliged to get alone with God and fight the battle out before Him. Until this is done, I lose every time. The battle may take one minute or a year; that will depend on me, not on God; but it must be wrestled out alone before God, and I must resolutely go through the hell of renunciation before God. . . . Every now and then . . . God brings us to . . . the Great Divide in life; from that point we either go towards a more and more dilatory and useless type of Christian life, or we become more and more ablaze for the glory of God.[2]

— OSWALD CHAMBERS

"What's the hardest thing for you ever, Mom?" Amy once asked me as she pored over her homework at the kitchen table, studying for a test that she was sure was going to be the hardest thing for her ever. As with all good questions, I don't remember my answer, only the question. What is the hardest thing for me ever?

I think it is to be true to what I know is right. Before I met Bill, I dated another young man. We were not only sweethearts but friends.

We loved the same writers, same music, and seemed to see the universe from the same perspective.

The years passed. I went to California and married Bill. The young man went to Vietnam and later went through a divorce. We kept in touch occasionally through Christmas cards, and at our twentieth high school reunion we saw each other again. The years evaporated, and it was as if we were kids again. The connection was surprisingly powerful, still there. I had never been tempted outside my marriage bonds before and was ambushed by strong emotions. I had the presence of mind to involve myself with other friends and family activities.

Later after I got home, he began to write. What was this? I reasoned with myself, "I love Bill; I wouldn't trade marriage to him and our family life for anything in the world."

I had an inner debate about answering the letters. I argued with myself, "It's just a friendship. We have so much in common. What's the harm of a simple correspondence, a friendship? Everybody needs friends."

But I knew it wasn't that simple. It was as if a magnet was pulling me away from all I knew that was good and honorable. And what was scary was that everything I knew to be right suddenly seemed dispensable, pale in comparison. I didn't feel at all spiritual, but I simply hung onto what I knew was right.

As I look back now, I see that I was at a vulnerable time and place. Since I married early, I had a lot of "what ifs" on my plate that needed to be examined. Too, Bill had been doing a lot of traveling, and I had a growing suspicion that my needs were not being met. (After all, aren't my needs important?) It is amazing how we justify disobedience on the basis of our needs. Jeremiah 17:9 puts it bluntly: "The heart is deceitful above all things, and desperately wicked. Who can know it?"

I was eventually able to talk about it with Bill, which helped me gain perspective. We needed to pay attention to what was going on in our own marriage, and this was a wake-up call. Rather than letting temptation drive a wedge in my commitments, I learned that it can be a strong reminder of what is truly important—to channel my emotions and energy in the right direction. Oswald Chambers, who was a chaplain in World War I and experienced great hardships, said, "If we are going to live as disciples of Jesus, we have to remember that all noble things are difficult. The Christian life is gloriously difficult, but the difficulty of it does not make us faint and cave in; it rouses us up to overcome."[3]

THE WAY OF ESCAPE

A young woman confessed to me that she was attracted to a married man. How could it be wrong, she wondered, when it felt so right? I was able to tell her with conviction and authority that just because she was attracted to him didn't make it right. Noted scholar F. B. Meyer wrote, "Consecration is not an act of our feeling, but of our will." Feelings are not the litmus test of truth—it is God's Word against which I can lean, knowing it will hold me.

We do not like to admit to such testing. But we must understand that it is not sin to be tempted. Jesus was tempted in all the ways we are, and He understands us. It is the response we make that determines whether the bearing wall will hold us or not. The good news is that the bearing wall in our lives—obedience to God's simple, righteous truth—is strong. It is straight and narrow, and when I lean against it, it holds.

James Dickey wrote, "We have all been in rooms we cannot die in."[4] The point is not to stay in the room you don't belong in—not to dwell there, to make it home. When we recognize this is a temptation from the enemy, it's time to get out of the room, to leave it. It is only when I throw myself on His mercy, knowing I cannot—of my own will—be holy, that I really do begin to comprehend what it means to be holy.

Living by our "feelings" is like trying to support a whole house and roof without a bearing wall. It can be a house of cards. Feelings are important because they tell us about ourselves, but they must not rule.

David, the lyricist and psalmist, the man after God's own heart, experienced this. In a midlife malaise, he looked next door and decided he knew best how to answer his own human hungers—through adultery with Bathsheba. The subtle decision to do things his own way eventually led to murder to cover his tracks. But notice when David repented with great tears and remorse, he prayed: "Against You, You only, have I sinned, and done this evil in Your sight" (Ps. 51:4). His sin affected his household—his own life, the life of his family, his nation. It had drastic consequences. But it was most personally a direct slam at the face of God. When everything is stripped away, the oldest temptation in the world, the one Eve gave in to, the same one her son Cain fell sway to is this: Does God know best? Or do I? Without doubt, "All we like sheep have gone astray" (Isa. 53:6). Plain and simple, all sin boils down to one thing—disobedience to the will of God.

There is a poignant scene in *Jane Eyre* when Rochester asked Jane to go away with him to the south of France. They loved each other, but he was a married man—married to an insane woman. To Jane, who had all her life dreamed of such love, the appeal was nearly irresistible. Only the memory of what she had been taught as a little girl saved her in that hour. Her response:

> Laws and principles are not for the time when there are no temptations; they are for such moments as this, when body and soul rise in mutiny against their rigor. Stringent are they; inviolate they shall be. If at my individual convenience I might break them, what would be their worth? They have a worth—so I have always believed; and if I cannot believe it now, it is because I am insane; with my veins running fire, and my heart beating faster than I can count its throbs. Here I plant my foot.[5]

Martin Luther, the great Reformation leader who stood up to his whole world and proclaimed salvation by faith rather than by works, declared, "Here I stand; I can do no otherwise. God help me. Amen!"[6]

What Holds Up My Life?

Just as bearing walls secure a house, what holds my life? I suppose you could rephrase that by asking, "What gives me the most security?" A title or position? Something I do? What I own or where I live?

Testing comes most sharply at the truest core of our humanity. It's important to understand where we are most vulnerable, to be sure we reinforce our lives at that point. I know that I am vulnerable to pressure. When I am plagued by deadlines, too much to do and not enough time, I begin to experience an inner panic and anxiety that spill over into the rest of my life. When I feel I am not living up to certain expectations (which is often), I tend to get down on myself. If I'm not careful, I slide into depression.

Not long ago I was in a "down" time—from overloading my "house" again. At the bottom of my depression, I prayed, "God, it is just so hard to live. I'm too tired; I am too much of a failure." Then in the quietness of His presence, it seemed His still, small voice said, "Just live for Me." So simple. My vulnerability—to live for others, to perform—is what must be addressed by the "bearing wall" of truth. He is the only one I must please. I'm learning that trust is the brace to keep my house strong.

Life can knock the stuffing out of us. Testing and temptation can surface in different ways and different places in our lives. It can be a pathway to fearful, dark thoughts. It can be an excuse to enter the soggy marsh of self-pity. Or simply the quest to "get even" that starts out looking like justice. Testing is an individual matter. But God promises, "No temptation has overtaken you except such as is common to man; but God is faithful, who will not allow you to be tempted beyond what you are able, but with the temptation will also make the way of escape, that you may be able to bear it" (1 Cor. 10:13).

Little Things Hold the Bearing Wall Together

It is, after all, so simple, I told myself. A house is nothing more than a collection of nails, thousands of them, driven—one after the other— each one, into a collection of wooden members, each one measured and cut, each after the other.[7]

—JOHN N. COLE

Webster defines a nail as "small thin metal fastener, a sharp metal object to attach things firmly." My father-in-law, a building contractor for many years, told me that certain frames call for certain kinds of nails, and in some places building codes require two nails to hold the pieces together. But if a builder is trying to hurry the job, he may skimp on the nails, which is detrimental to the building. The little things that hold up the bearing wall and the rest of the framing— the nails—are absolutely essential.

Some small things are pretty important, when you think about it. Small battles can win big wars. Every good, righteous life is a myriad of small decisions to do the right thing. And every life of transgression begins with entertaining a single thought, a justification of an action. It's all well and good to say, "Just do the right thing. Don't yield to temptation, to what you know is destructive." Sometimes it takes more than a slogan—it takes a well-driven fastener, adhering to the "code"—to hold the frame together. Ecclesiastes 12:11 says, "The words of the wise are like goads, and the words of scholars are like well-driven nails, given by one Shepherd."

Often it is the little things, the undramatic things, the invisible things that hold a life, a family, a church, a nation together. A man who built his entire house with his own hands wrote about his experience:

> When you build a house, you'll pound several kegs (of nails), and when you finish, you'll hardly remember a single one. Spread over the days, nails aren't that memorable; measured against the glory of your own shelter, they evaporate like dewdrops in the midday sun. You may live a year with the travail of shelter-building; you will live a lifetime with the blazing knowledge of your accomplishment.[8]

Revelation 3:2 says to "strengthen the things which remain." What remains? What "nail" holds you together? Thank God for that thread of commitment, of continuity—the single well-driven nail; hang onto it. Together with many other vital small connectors, this may be the link that holds your house up.

It may be a tradition such as Sunday dinner at the relatives or attending family reunions. An important, honest friendship with someone who is not impressed by you. The simple commitment of being in church, though you may not feel like being there. Taking Communion, remembering what it's all about. Personal devotions, retreats. Family prayers. These "little things" help to strengthen the commitments in our lives, to make real what we know.

> *I have come back again to where I belong;*
> *not an enchanted place, but the walls are strong.*[9]
>
> – DOROTHY H. RATH

Forging your house for God with sturdy walls is not easy, and if anyone says it is, I question his or her experience. Just like building a house, building a life can be discouraging, mind-numbing work. Things go wrong. The weather may not cooperate.

Our neighbors are building a house this winter, and they've had several frustrating delays due to rain and snow. But they're forging ahead, and little by little the house is progressing. It will be beautiful when it's completed, and surely it can't rain forever (although sometimes it seems like it here in the Northwest)! No—if you're building a truly great project, you press on with the dream of what can be. And once the house is completed, you'd think, *What if I'd quit back there when it was so rough? I would have missed this!*

Scott Peck writes, "The truth is that our finest moments, more often than not, occur precisely when we are uncomfortable, when we're not feeling happy or fulfilled, when we're struggling and searching."[10]

We must not be afraid of the testing places. They will come. Alan Jones wrote, "We can't help being lovers, and we go astray in our loving in three ways: by loving the wrong things, by not loving the right things enough, and by loving certain things too much. Our loving needs ordering. Our desiring needs educating. Both love and desire can easily go off in the wrong direction and be turned into hate."[11]

Herein lies our Gethsemane—where we honestly look at our need. And make no mistake—our needs, our wants feel very real. But when we can say, "God, You promised to meet my every need according to Your riches in glory," He does meet us. And rather than this being a place of defeat, it can be a place of victory. Walking with an awareness of our humanity actually makes us stronger, more compassionate, more truly able to minister God's grace because we've experienced it.

The storms and questioning and uncertainty never stop, and we must make sure we are building with material that will hold fast. Testing is a necessary part of life. It is that very pressure, however, that reveals the beauty and strength of the bearing wall—the truth of Jesus Christ.

Learn from the Builder

When the builder of a house understands the structural loads, how to identify weak points in a house design, it is possible avoid to disaster later. One builder listed four principles[12] to build a solid house that I believe apply to our lives as well:

1. *Anticipate the possible loads that each part of the house may have to carry, and design accordingly.* How much can I carry? Is it possible that I'm setting myself up for greater temptation by my lifestyle? Where are my weak points, my vulnerabilities, and how can I fortify these areas?

2. *Mentally go through the house design, making sure all joints and connections are strong enough, braced and stable.* Do I need to increase accountability relationships or support systems that will give me balance in my life?

3. *When in doubt, design the structure twice as strong as you think it needs to be (strong is more important than pretty).* An ounce of prevention is worth a pound of cure. I can structure my life to avoid unnecessary testing. Let form follow function.

4. *Learn to "see" how forces are transmitted through a structure. Visualize what could happen with certain stresses, and then reinforce it.* Think it through: If I were to give in to temptation, what would be the result? Think consequences. Imagine what could happen if I give in, and be realistic—don't sugarcoat the entire consequences. Allow yourself to feel the emotions that such a disaster would bring.

Trust

When I was speaking at a weekend retreat in Florida, a woman told me about the intense testing she was experiencing. She had done her best to raise her son in their Christian family, but when he reached his teens, he went into complete rebellion, using drugs and alcohol. The family had tried everything to turn him around, and still his life was chaos. She said, her eyes brimming, "I know God said He would not tempt us above what we are able, but I'm beginning to wonder." I had no magic solution for her. I simply held her hand and listened to her and encouraged her to hold onto what she knew, that sometimes the answer is not immediate. It is at such times that we must trust the character of God and trust His Word. I am continually reminded when I speak to people from all walks of life that regardless of their position, everyone (if we are honest) has moments of crushing pressure.

Bear with One Another

Just as the bearing wall is reinforced by other walls and braces, we need people who know us, who are not afraid to tell us the truth. We also need one another simply for comfort. One of my favorite theologians, Winnie the Pooh, was walking down the road one day when Piglet sidled up to him and took his paw.

"Pooh?" Piglet said.

"Yes, Piglet?" Pooh questioned.

"Nothing," Piglet answered, holding his paw. "I just wanted to be sure of you."[13]

Sometimes it's enough just to be "on the road" with someone, side by side, not necessarily with any answers. In offering our presence, we fulfill the law of Christ. It is a powerful gift we can give one another, to help one another through difficult places. It can be a helpless feeling to not have any answers. It's much easier to ride in with a sheaf full of solutions, and yet our very helplessness, our not knowing what to say, can be a comfort and strength.

A friend who was going through unbelievable pressure spent a weekend with us, and she spent a lot of time talking. Her situation was very complicated and painful, and Bill and I had no solutions.

There was really nothing we could say. When she left, I felt we hadn't helped her at all. Months later I saw her, glowing with God's provision and sustenance, and she thanked us for our "help." We had done nothing—we had simply listened to her. It affirmed something to me: Most of us know what is right. At some of our most difficult times, we just need someone to stand shoulder-to-shoulder with us.

The honest concern of another is a powerful antidote to testing, to help keep us standing true. Unfortunately, it's often at our weakest places we are most afraid to open up and ask for prayer and support, perhaps because we are afraid of being judged. When fellow believers face illness and death, it's easy to flood them with cards and meals and flowers. But when other situations, such as divorce or disgrace happen—we can become silent, distant. We privately judge, or feel judged—at the time when we most need one another. Galatians 6:2 says, "Bear one another's burdens, and so fulfill the law of Christ."

We were vacationing in the San Juan Islands and got off our boat to explore an island where lumber and mining entrepreneurs had free reign in the 1800s. As we walked across the island, we came upon a large old house that one of the early lumber barons had built on a bluff overlooking the bay. We studied the house, struck by its charm. Someone had obviously built with great imagination and flair, but the house was now ready to fall down. The porch sagged. The foundation was starting to crumble.

The sun shone brilliantly as we walked around the deserted house, the sea and islands breathtakingly beautiful in the distance. Butterflies and bumblebees touched down on the hollyhocks and lilac bushes that still bloomed in front of the house. This was a real home once. Real people worked, lived, and raised children here, and it was apparent that they loved beauty, by the location and design of the house. Through a side window, we saw a stairway that looked ready to cave in. The house itself seemed to list to one side, and even though there were many fine details, it was obvious that this house was very fragile. It appeared that the house had never really been reinforced with strong bearing walls and a good foundation. Beautiful and unique as the house once was, it was now crumbling, apparently beyond repair.

As I looked at this house that had once been beautiful and productive, I thought of another older home I had toured in Portland that had been built the same year. Both houses had been built with the best of intentions. Both were originally beautiful. The house in Portland, however, had been strongly reinforced and maintained through the years. Time had made it even more beautiful. But the house standing before me was a poignant reminder of what could have been. I took a deep breath and walked away, thinking about my own life—about what keeps me strong.

I know it is the bearing wall of truth, and I must continually keep it before me, leaning on it always.

YOUR TESTING PLACES

∽ If you feel you are in a "testing place" now, consider: What principle, what part of my character is being tested? What's at stake?

∽ For further study read Ephesians 6; 2 Corinthians 7:1; Hebrews 12; Hebrews 4:14-16; John 3:6-10; Psalm 16:11

∽

Lord, here I sit again at my little place of prayer with my Bible on this quiet morning. As I consider my own "house for God," at times it seems so fragile and too often a "house for self." Father, forgive me for wanting things that are not good for me, for looking for the path of least resistance. Help me not to fear testing, but to welcome it, and in the testing, lean hard on You.

O God, my heart is fixed—there is no one like You! Empty me of selfishness, pride, hostility, fear. Replace it with the loveliness of Christ. Be Lord of me—my house. Create in me a clean heart, O God, and renew a right spirit within me.

And, Father, show me what it means to be separated, holy unto You. Amen.

❧

My Personal Reflections

_____

_____

_____

_____

_____

_____

_____

_____

_____

_____

_____

_____

_____

_____

Six

⌘

INFRASTRUCTURE

⌘

*I am the vine, you are the branches. He who abides in Me, and I
in him, bears much fruit; for without Me you can do nothing.*

—JOHN 15:5

The beautiful bare walls were up now, nailed securely in place, and Bill
and his father were pleased with the progress of the house. This house
was looking good. As we prepared now for the plumbing and electrical work, we soon discovered that it would be best to use the designs
and skills of professionals. After all, power is nothing to take lightly.
You can't just dabble at it and have it really work for you. Bill winced
slightly as he watched his handiwork marred by drills and saws so that
the necessary wires and pipes could go through the entire house.

The wires were threaded through each room, and the electrician
knew where to put the outlets. The plumbing—similar in many
ways to electrical wiring—got attention too; soon fresh water would
be able to flow into the house for drinking, bathing, cooking, and
washing. Drainage pipes were installed to allow for the used water
and waste to leave the house. Heating ducts and vents had to be
roughed in as well. Before long the naked wires and pipes were covered with insulation, then Sheetrock and paint, and the power of the
house was hidden—yet accessible when needed.

My eyes glazed over when discussing wiring, plumbing, and

energy systems with Bill and the subcontractors. I was eager to get on to what I considered the fun part—painting, wallpapering, and decorating. However, the more I got into this phase of building, the more I realized that the infrastructure—the guts of the house—had to be one of the most important aspects of the entire building project. After all, I wanted a house that worked. Even the most primitive house uses some kind of energy to make living easier.

I know what it's like not to have electricity, water, or heat. Several years ago in a major snowstorm, our electricity was out for several days. We also had frozen pipes, so we had no water. After a few hours, the romance of the fireplace (inadequate to heat our entire house), cooking over a propane stove, and hauling water grew thin. How I took my daily comforts for granted, I thought wryly. I was immensely relieved when the power came back on. All I had to do was turn a switch, and the lights came on. Open the faucet, and water poured out. Flip the lever, and the heat came on. An amazing miracle I enjoy every day, hardly stopping to think about it. No, I don't understand the infrastructure's complexities, but that doesn't stop me from using it.

MY SOURCE OF POWER

> *But the Lord said to her, "My dear Martha, you are so upset over all these details! There is really only one thing worth being concerned about. Mary has discovered it—and I won't take it away from her."*
>
> — LUKE 10:41-42 NLT

I want my life to work, too. Like you, I want my life to make a difference, and I want my giving to be meaningful. But how does that happen?

Quality material for the inside helps make a quality house—

materials worth choosing, because in the long run, this is what makes a worthy, solid house that will endure. And so I must give thought to what I'm building inside my life, too. I must make sure I rely on God's excellence and the power of His Holy Spirit for the all-important work of the infrastructure.

Shortly after Bill and I married, both of us were working full time, and even though we were involved in ministry, I didn't take time for personal Bible study and prayer. Time to think, to study, to know my own mind just didn't fit into my life then. Instead, I lived vicariously off others' spiritual experiences, consumed as I was with my job, my new marriage, and with living in the city—a place I found fascinating.

One evening we were at a friend's house for a gathering, and during a lull in the conversation, the leader of the group turned to me and in front of everyone said, "Nancie, why don't you share what God is doing in your life?" I gulped. I hated that word *share*. What did I have to share anyway? Frankly, I didn't have anything to "share," and I should have said so. Instead, I gave some phony response, my face burning with embarrassment.

Sure, I had a secure foundation—a healthy frame; I was just spiritually barren inside. How does someone develop the inside of a life—a life filled with the power of God, a life of passion and purpose that bears fruit—especially if her life is like mine? How do I actually plug into God's power? It seemed to me that saints—at least the ones with Profound and Great Thoughts—were all dead or celibate or preachers in a pulpit. Here I was, slugging it out in real life. Could God's power really impact my life?

The question my friend innocently asked was the beginning of a tentative journey to see what was inside, and the first step was truth. I saw that I was not growing; I was not honestly seeking after God to really know Him. I just wanted Him for what He could give me to make my life better. Humbled, I began to look for quiet moments to seek God, often finding them unexpectedly and surprisingly.

Finding my Source and plugging into Him took persistence and creativity. When I had small children, I rarely had time to sit down, yet I kept my Bible open on the kitchen counter to snatch a verse or two on the run. It was a ragged start, but I'm relieved that God met me exactly where I was—at a place of asking. It was only later that I learned to welcome brokenness and emptiness, something I used to avoid at all costs.

Life doesn't stop and wait for us to grow deep. It pushes us along with our jobs and commitments and family cares, and it's easy to be caught up in the very real demands of life. It's as if you're living in a big house—kitchen, bedrooms, and bathrooms, the living area all there—but with no energy. Everything may seem to be there, but if it's not hooked up to fresh water, plugged into light and heat that make the house really alive, it's not a house that's living up to its potential to meet human needs. Jesus freely offers us His power to live, to overcome. He said to the woman at the well, "If you only knew the gift God has for you and who I am, you would ask me, and I would give you living water. . . . The water I give them takes away thirst altogether. It becomes a perpetual spring within them, giving them eternal life" (John 4:10, 14 NLT).

And when Jesus left earth to go back to the Father, He sent the Comforter, the Holy Spirit, to us. Jesus told His disciples, "I will send you the Counselor—the Spirit of truth. He will come to you from the Father and will tell you all about me" (John 15:26 NLT).

I learned to find the still, quiet places to begin the pursuit to know Him, to get in touch with God's power for my life, my real life. As a wife and mother of five, it was easy to be so consumed by my family's immediate needs that I forgot that ultimately it is my soul, my own life that I must account for. It's not just a hobby for the religiously inclined. It is necessary to pursue God to truly live—because only when I truly know God's love can I genuinely love. Only when I am listened to, can I really listen. Solitude is necessary because out of it I see the essential, "needful thing" that Jesus told Mary about in Luke 10. But this priority does not come to me. I must seek it out, make time for it.

THE IMPORTANT IS OFTEN HIDDEN

Hasten unto Him who calls you in the silences of your hearts.[1]

—THOMAS R. KELLY

Certain hidden things—such as the wiring and plumbing of a house—are extremely powerful. The psalmist talked about "hiding" God's Word in our hearts to guard against sin (Ps. 119:11). Isaiah 45:3 says, "I will give you the treasures of darkness and hidden riches of secret places, that you may know that I, the LORD, who call you by your name, am the God of Israel." Peter instructed women on the essentials: "Let [your adorning] be the hidden person of the heart, with the incorruptible beauty of a gentle and quiet spirit" (1 Peter 3:4). Hidden things can be powerful.

A "hidden life" with God is a discipline, a habit that doesn't come easily. It isn't written into my day-timer. Most often my family members don't even see me when I am praying and studying. This part of my life is solitary, hidden. And yet it is out of this life that my real life works, because this is where I've learned to tap into real power. These three simple disciplines have helped me:

1. *I learned to journal my prayers.* I found the journal to be a safe place for me—a place where I can be gut-level honest as I seek God's purpose and direction for my life, a place where I dare to write my anger and fears and joys and then invite God into those very places,

applying Scripture to them. David, the man after God's own heart, is an example of allowing God fully into his weaknesses and pain. That was the strength of his spiritual life and the reason for the incredible ministry of the Psalms throughout the centuries. Countless people have benefited because of their honesty and assurance of God's presence in the absolute depths of despair as well as in heights of joy.

2. *I learned to have a consistent study of God's Word.* In addition to private study, I've found it helpful to be in a small group Bible study because in this setting I was able to actually discuss the biblical principles that were causing change in my life. It's important to be committed to obey God's Word, to actually apply its teachings to my life, to ponder it as I go through ordinary days. There are times I am not able to be in a Bible study, and I miss it. But this increases the value of journaling, because later I can read back and actually see my response to struggles and what I was learning in Scripture about them.

3. *I've learned the importance of waiting on God—to go about my life being prayerful.* I'm learning to praise Him more and not complain so much. I found that I was doing a lot of "moaning" to God, and even though I prayed earnestly, I worried even more earnestly. I saw a big change in my prayers when I began to praise Him and live with an awareness of Him, of His awesome power. It's possible to pray in the very "process" of life, to pray without ceasing—while car-pooling, waiting in line at the grocery checkout, before falling asleep at night. God comes to us as we invite Him, just where we are. It's a heart attitude, an inward stance of listening to Him, responding to others as He would.

> Lord, let my life be orderly, regular, temperate; let no pride or self-
> seeking, no covetousness or revenge, no little ends and low imagi-

nations pollute my spirit and unhallow my words and actions. Let my body be a servant of my spirit and both my body and spirit be servants of Jesus, doing all things for your glory here. Amen.

— JEREMY TAYLOR

THE HOUSE COMES ALIVE

When He, the Spirit of truth, has come, He will guide you into all truth; for He will not speak on His own authority, but whatever He hears He will speak; and He will tell you things to come. He will glorify Me, for He will take of what is Mine and declare it to you.

— JOHN 16:13-14

The wiring was finally finished in the construction of our house. It was winter—stormy and cold outside—and up to this time, the electrician had used portable lighting because the shorter days made the inside of the house dark. One wonderful afternoon all the wiring was connected, and we simply turned on the lights. Our house was illumined; it was beautiful. We stood in awe as the snow piled up deep outside. The light showcased our house that we'd planned and dreamed and worked so hard for. Now we could really see it, appreciate it. The house came alive only because the electrician used the right wiring and wired it according to the code, connecting it to the source. He did it right.

There is a cost to doing it right. Yes, Jesus seeks us out, but we must submit ourselves to God. It is also true that the Holy Spirit showcases Jesus. Scripture is clear: The Holy Spirit came to put the spotlight on Jesus, our Redeemer, the one who came to seek us out, to restore us and bring our lives true fulfillment. The one who discerns our hearts and deepest motives and yet cares for us as a shepherd. Jesus' words confront us to the core of our lives, and we must respond to Him.

Jesus told His disciples in the upper room, "Abide in me. . . . I am the vine, you are the branches" (John 15:5). Learning how to simply be the branch plugging into His power is so simple it's difficult. Why? Because it requires surrender.

There are many distractions keeping us from listening to Him, and we tenaciously latch onto them—good, worthy distractions that we all have—making a living, social events, church activities, busy-ness, the television that blares nonsense and mediocrity and consumes too much of my thought, my own needs (which seem extremely urgent). Most of all, my independence that keeps me thinking *I can handle this situation, this problem. I'll figure this out.* As Jesus told Martha, "Martha . . . you are worried and troubled about many things." Indeed.

The other day in my devotions I prayed sincerely, "Lord, be so at home in me that when others are near me, they sense Your presence." Not twenty minutes after I prayed this, I made a rude comment to someone, a completely uncalled-for reaction. Suddenly I understood—I cannot; He can. The key to plugging into His power is to understand my complete helplessness without Him. To love through Him, because of Him, not anything I manufacture. I am a shell without His presence. No light, no heat, no real love. Yes, I am a house, but without Him, I am nothing. He is the vine, I am a branch. He is my source of power.

I desperately need the power of the Holy Spirit because life can become so unbelievably complex, and I need His guidance. After all, that is one of His functions—to come alongside us, to lead us into truth. There are situations that cannot be readily solved in a counselor's office. This book you are reading will not solve all your problems (although I would love to think it could point you to the one who can). Sometimes relationships can be impossible, decisions complicated. This is when the Holy Spirit can speak to us and lead us if we are willing to wait, to listen, to respond.

THE RESULTS OF POWER: FRUIT

> *Saints . . . are ordinary people who are inwardly attending to the*
> *highest truth they know and who are prepared to let this truth have*
> *undivided sway in their lives. . . . [They] are not afraid of conse-*
> *quences because they are such avid lovers of the truth they have*
> *found.*[2]
>
> —DOUGLAS V. STEERE

Jesus wants us to bear fruit—to love others as He loved us, to be His servants, His ministers. "Bear much fruit," Jesus instructed. His light, His power, His cleansing (like the infrastructure of my house) are given to us for a reason—that we would bear fruit and reflect Him. I have much to learn about respecting the "power" in my house. It's not mine to play games with nor to abuse. I must respect it and use it as the need arises. Just as a house needs to be "energy efficient," I must be, too!

Bearing fruit is not a "doing" thing; it's a "being" thing. Jesus told His disciples before He left them, "You shall receive power when the Holy Spirit has come upon you; and you shall be witnesses to Me in Jerusalem, and in all Judea and Samaria, and to the end of the earth" (Acts 1:8). It's interesting that Jesus said His disciples would be witnesses, not do witnessing. I've found it's much easier to "do" Christianity—attend all the church services, be involved in all the programs, go to meetings, and do everything I think a Christian should do. But when do I really start bearing fruit? Real fruit—fruit that remains? Much fruit, as Jesus said, takes pruning, stripping away, submitting to His plan and purpose in my life, which can be painful and uncomfortable. Plugging into Him as my source takes much prayer, much listening, much reliance on Him—and a clear understanding of my weakness and a sharper realization that His yoke is easy and His burden is light.

I have seen the results of the Holy Spirit's power in people's lives. I have seen it intimately in the lives of my mother and father. Even now I see the power of God in the prayer-filled lives of my mother-in-law and father-in-law, who daily pray for countless family members and friends. Their prayers have been a hedge around our family. I have seen God's presence bring hope to a young widow who was devastated by the death of her husband, leaving her with a young family and no steady income.

I have sensed the Holy Spirit in many worship services, through praise and through the pastor's faithful teaching of God's Word.

God used me at a moment when I did not expect it. Occasionally we have foreign exchange students live with us, and Dorli, an attractive young university student from Austria, stayed with us one winter a few years ago. One evening we were at a basketball game at a local high school watching one of our sons play. A friend of mine was very ill in the hospital, which happened to be near the school. At halftime I leaned over and told our family I intended to run up to Lily's room just for a moment to pray for her. Dorli impulsively said, "I'm going with you."

We went from a noisy gym into the quiet, darkened room where Lily was lying so very ill. I simply held Lily's hand, hugged her, and prayed briefly and rather helplessly for her. Dorli and I told her good-bye and went back to our basketball game. (I'm sad to say that Lily died a few weeks later.)

Shortly before Dorli went back to Austria, she came into my room one day and said, "Remember when we went up to see Lily, and you prayed? Can you just talk to God like that? Would you teach me how?"

I was amazed and overjoyed to tell her, "Yes, you can talk to God just like that! And I would be delighted to teach you. It is so simple." Dorli had seen that night in Lily's hospital room within two very frail human vessels—mine and Lily's—something very powerful: God's presence.

I have sensed the Holy Spirit very keenly during some of our prison conferences that we do inside the Oregon State Women's Penitentiary. I have a hunch it has to do with our team's prayer and fasting, my sense of utter helplessness and dependence upon God. Too, many women inside are ready for some real answers.

One Saturday night stands out in my mind. Most of the women were chain-smokers, and the smell permeated everything inside, the ashtrays overflowing. I was leading the singing, and they were singing one of their favorites: "Do, Lord, O do, Lord, O do remember me . . ." They sang it heartily, I thought, maybe pleadingly. (*Don't forget me when You go, okay? O Lord, do You see me? Please remember me.*)

I looked around the room. Many of the women had tattoos, scars, their faces lined from stress, from anger, from grief. A few were beautiful. Most were young and touched indelibly by the worst of what life offers. And then we began to sing, "Amazing grace, how sweet the sound that saved a wretch like me." The miracle happened. How can I explain it? Only that the Holy Spirit was in that room, and grace began to touch the women's lives. It touched their faces as they sang, softened them, and made them beautiful, young. Tears poured down their faces—mine, too—as we sensed the healing love of Jesus pouring through all the fibers of our being: "Neither do I condemn you—go and sin no more." "I give you living water." "Peace I give unto you." "I will never leave you nor forsake you."

That night many women made decisions to accept Christ into their lives. I thought of the penitent thief hanging on the cross beside Jesus, asking Him, "Lord, remember me when You come into Your kingdom." And Jesus assured him he would be with Him that very day.

Could it be that His Spirit indeed is in the prisons—the out-of-the-way places where poverty has crushed people? That He is with the disenfranchised, the forgotten? And when we touch these in His name, He places His hand over ours and says, "I am here, too."

Scripture urges us to "have faith in God." Jesus said, "Blessed are they that have not seen, yet believe." How do we have faith? We trust the object of our faith—God. One of our family's favorite hymns is "Great Is Thy Faithfulness." God's faithfulness is what I can trust, because He never fails. Jesus said, "If you have faith as a grain of mustard seed." A mustard seed is tiny. Sometimes we think we have to be giants in faith. We don't! Faith is a simple step toward God. Hebrews says, "He who comes to God must believe that He is, and that He is a rewarder of those who diligently seek Him" (11:6).

My daughter Amy asked me the other day, "But, Mom, how do we know there is a heaven? How do we know that we will see Grandma and Grandpa someday?" I told her, "Amy, it is faith. And faith sometimes includes acknowledging our questions, our doubts." After all, the father who came to Jesus with his desperately sick boy said, "Lord, I believe! But help my unbelief." The thing is, He came to Jesus—even with his doubts. I asked Amy, "Do you completely understand how this light switch works to light the kitchen?" "No," she answered. "But I still turn it on. It works."

Being "plugged into" the power of God through the Holy Spirit is not some sort of mystical experience reserved for the very spiritual. It is simply an awareness of my emptiness without Him—that He is my strength, my shield. Yes, it is a mystery. I don't fully understand it. I only know He is the source of real life, and I must cling to Him, trust Him with all my heart. He is light, and He is truth, and by faith I invite Him to shine His light on the innermost rooms of my heart.

> Trust not nor lean upon a reed shaken by the wind; for that all flesh
> is grass, and all the glory thereof shall wither away as the flower of

the field. Thou wilt soon be deceived, if thou only look to the outward appearance of men. For, if thou seekest thy comfort and thy profit in others, thou shall often feel loss. If thou seekest Jesus in all things, thou shalt surely find Jesus. But if thou seekest thyself, thou shall also find thyself, but to thine own destruction.[3]

—THOMAS À KEMPIS

YOUR HOUSE COMES ALIVE

❧ What in your life can only be explained by the power of God? Is He your source for living?

❧ For further study read John 15. Read Galatians 5 and consider for your own life what it means to be filled with the Holy Spirit.

❧

Lord, so often I am distracted when I come into Your presence. You have given me much—good people to love, worthy commitments to keep. Sometimes I forget and think I am the one who must solve the problems, find the solutions.

Help me to know the source of my strength—You, Father. I am destitute, useless without You. May I rest in Your strength, move in Your power. May I not get ahead of You, but learn instead to wait upon You. And in the waiting, may I understand what it means to live and move and have my very being in You. In Jesus' strong name. Amen.

❧

My Personal Reflections

_____

_____

_____

_____

_____

*S*even

❧

WINDOWS
IN MY HOUSE

❧

He who has a generous eye will be blessed.

— PROVERBS 22:9

When Bill designed our house, he gave the windows careful thought. While windows have the practical function of letting in light, warmth, and air, they also give a house its unique flavor, its personality. Windows can make a house.

Bill made sure most of our windows were set into the side of the house that faced the morning sun, away from the street. This way, our house opens onto trees and grass and gives us privacy and a pleasant view. We often have deer, raccoons, squirrels, and porcupines in our yard as well as an occasional coyote. A bird feeder in a tree outside our living room window lets us watch a variety of birds. Through our windows we have an ever-changing, interesting view and a sense of being outside. Too, the southern exposure takes advantage of winter sun to help heat the house.

Although our bedrooms have curtains and shades, we decided not to put any covering on the large windows in our living room, kitchen, and dining room except for wooden crosspieces that are on all the windows and doors. This very moment I am sitting in my favorite studying place, a love seat next to the bay window in my kitchen. I am a fanatic about windows; I like big, wide ones open to the light.

> *I remember, I remember*
> *The house where I was born,*
> *The little window where the sun*
> *Came peeping in at morn.*[1]

When I was nine, my parents began to do a significant remodeling job on our old farmhouse. The house had been built out on the northern Montana prairie in 1910 as a refuge from the blast of winter storms and wind that swept down from the Rocky Mountains. After all, when you're out working the land, you come inside for food and shelter, not to take advantage of the panoramic view. Big windows would have made heating the house even more difficult, so the windows were small. There was a large porch in front of the house facing the mountains, but the only time the weather permitted us to sit there to enjoy the view was in summer, and then the mosquitoes were so bad nobody could stand it.

So it was a big deal for us when my father got rid of the old oil furnace and put in a new heating system so we could have "picture windows" installed in the expanded living room. It made a dramatic difference, and finally we could look at the mountains from inside our house. We had an open house for the neighbors to show off the results.

Windows are wonderful inventions. They speak to me of the human quality of perspective that each of us has—a point of view. We all have a "view" of things, and our outlook on life powerfully influences the rest of our lives.

WHERE YOU ARE DETERMINES WHAT YOU SEE

> *Thou that hast given so much to me,*
> *Give me one thing more—a grateful heart;*

Not thankful when it pleaseth me,
As if Thy blessings had spare days;
But such a heart, whose pulse may be Thy praise.[2]

—GEORGE HERBERT

My view changes as my life changes. My first home as a married woman was an apartment in San Francisco. I remember looking out my kitchen window to watch the ever-changing sky over the bay, and I loved seeing the pastel-colored houses, row upon row. I saw the city as intriguing, exciting, and grew used to the constant sound of sirens. I was not afraid—the city beckoned to me. But as years went by and I became a mother, I began to see the world differently. Now I wanted houses with yards and swing sets, safe neighborhoods for my children to play in.

Not long ago I finished the rough draft for this book at a room on the Oregon Coast. I remembered vacationing in the same area twenty years ago with Bill and our small children. We'd needed to leave the little beach house clean for its next occupants, and since we had two cars, I stayed to clean the house, and Bill and the children went on home ahead of me.

My trip home was interrupted in a small town where traffic was sealed off because of a parade. I found myself stranded in a community where everyone knew everyone else. I gave up trying to get through town, bought myself a snow cone, and settled down to watch the parade with the rest of the folk. It was the oddest sensation to be alone when everyone else seemed to know each other. I felt invisible and conspicuous at the same time. I realized anew: When you are part of a family, you see life from that "window." When you are the other half of a couple, you see life from that window. When you are part of a particular organization or denomination, you see life from that window. At the time I got stuck in the middle of that parade, my window on life was that of a young wife and mother.

If you'd told me then that twenty years later I would be seeking out five days of solitude at the beach, I would not have believed it nor understood it. I rarely had a moment alone in the bathroom, not to mention anywhere else. I could not have related to the idea of deliberately driving by myself somewhere to be by myself! But now I desperately needed the solitude—and a room with a view—to work on my book.

Why would I leave home with its pleasant views to work on this project? Because I needed a fresh perspective, and I needed to focus. A change of scenery can be healthy, bring new insights. That very brief interlude twenty years ago in a coastal town watching a parade by myself reminded me to be more aware of my single friends, to remember to include them in our family life. Seeing life from the other person's point of view enlarges one's vision. It can be easy to have tunnel vision if we are never exposed to other perspectives, if we never even take the time to look.

HOW BIG ARE YOUR WINDOWS?

> *I will hew great windows, wonderful windows, measureless windows for my soul.*[3]

> —ANGELA MORGAN

Big windows help us see better, give us a wider perspective. They also make our house seem bigger, more expansive, more accommodating. If we have a narrow point of view on certain situations, we can have a restricted, narrow vision. We see less. A person who is prejudiced has a narrow view of others.

But it's not just the size of the view—our perspective; it's what I choose to notice out my window. I remember being ecstatic to be back at the ocean for this concentrated time of writing, and when I checked into my room, the first thing I did was fling open the shades. Yes, there was the wonderful Pacific Ocean, but over two rooftops. I set up the computer, organized my material, and got ready to write about windows, not liking what I saw out my window. *What is the matter with you? Why are you acting like a spoiled brat?* I asked myself. I'd planned this trip for so long, looked forward to it with such anticipation, and here I was, fuming over two rooftops. No matter that the room was clean and comfortable and the ocean wide and beckoning.

I began to realize that it wasn't my surroundings that bothered me; it was me. As surely as I lugged up books, my computer, and coffeepot, I also lugged up my troubles in a big invisible bag. The distractions weren't external; they were internal (nagging, chronic worries . . . my growing children—are they making the right choices? Amy lost another contact lens. . . . Whatever am I going to say when I speak next week to those women? . . . Can I possibly get this book written and write something meaningful?).

It's not so much the window. Sure, the scenery changes from time to time depending on where I am in life, but it's what I choose to notice out my window. We all know people who see the glass as half-full rather than half-empty. I tend to be a half-empty person and have to work hard at being positive. I have a melancholy streak which, if I don't rein in, has me seeing everything in shades of gray.

It's what's inside of us that determines what we notice. Have you ever heard two people describing the same situation differently? Not long ago Bill and I were at a conference listening to a husband-and-wife team speak about their years of pastoring. He taught the first session, warmly telling of their successes and victories. His wife stood up to teach the second session and smilingly asked her husband, "Was that the same church I was in?" She had a different view of it.

The wife would argue (and I would agree with her) that his view of things was unrealistic, that he chose not to see some things. And he would be right to say there were many positives—why not focus on them instead of on the negative? And how is it that siblings can have such differing views of their parents? We do see things differently, depending upon our perspective—and we can choose how we see certain things. We have a lot to say about the size and position of our windows on life and circumstances that come our way.

WHAT IS MY RESPONSE TO WHAT I SEE?

> *Whenever I am afraid, I will trust in You.*
>
> — PSALM 56:3

When I was very small, I watched a terrifying thunderstorm outside my bedroom window. The trees tossed in the wind, and I saw lightning strike a cottonwood tree, splitting it with a ball of fire. It was ferocious and scary. But I felt safe inside near my parents as I snuggled in bed.

My son and daughter-in-law have an elderly neighbor next door to them who keeps every shade completely drawn in her house, even though she has some wonderful views. I don't know her, but I get the impression she is afraid. If so, I can empathize. As I began to have children, I suddenly saw the world as a dangerous place from which I needed to protect my children. My worries and fears got so bad I was afraid to stay alone, afraid to drive, and my life was becoming paralyzed by fear.

I finally realized I had to saturate myself with God's Word to counteract the fear, and God has helped me immensely in this area. But I've found that each new area of life offers opportunities to be afraid. Psalm 94:19 says, "In the multitude of my anxieties within me, Your comforts delight my soul." That's exactly what anxieties can become if left unchecked—multitudes. Fear is creative, and given free rein, it grows. Yet each new area of life, each new place offers opportunities to see with eyes of faith rather than fear. The way out of fear, I believe, is learning the discipline of having a grateful heart, to see with faith rather than with fear.

Is it scary outside my window? Figuratively speaking, you bet it is. There are more opportunities to be afraid than I can count. And the potential for fear increases with time. The world can be terrifying as I look at the storms raging outside (culturally and spiritually), sometimes striking very close to my house.

It isn't natural for me to have a grateful perspective. It's taking me a lifetime to develop an attitude that says, "Thank You, God. I believe You are with me, and You have everything under control." I'm finding that this is not a trivial mind game. It's really a profound statement of faith.

Holding onto my fears and pessimistic thinking is a control issue. It's trying to assert that I have some control over events, people, circumstances. I don't. All I have control over is my attitude—what I think about, how I choose to see people and situations. I must say (sometimes over and over in my mind) to my children, to other situations that consume my thinking: "I choose to trust God with you."

Our son Chris has a unique characteristic: He has a sky-blue eye and a chocolate-brown one. From the time Chris was very small, we would tell him, "God has made you very special. That is your unique trademark." Maybe we overdid the "special" angle. Years ago as I was driving, I told Chris, who was bouncing in the backseat without his seat belt, to sit down and buckle himself in.

He did so but protested, "Well, Mom, God wouldn't let anything happen to me, would He? His special boy with the blue eye and the brown eye?"

I smiled, but it made me think. Often this has been my reasoning: God wouldn't let anything happen to me, would He? If I did all the right things—memorized the key Scriptures, read the right books—everything would fall into place, and I would get what I deserved in life. Wouldn't I? Shouldn't I? Nothing terrible would happen to me.

Well . . . nothing, except life!

Not long ago I interviewed Barbara Johnson for *Virtue* magazine. Barbara, a popular speaker, has written many books about her response to tragedy in her life. Two of her four sons were killed, and one of her sons got into the gay lifestyle. Her message—not of denial but of humor and of reaching out to other parents who suffer loss and disappointment—gets a phenomenal response from others. She is one of the most upbeat, positive women I know, and she's an inspiration to thousands. You may say, "What I see in my life is not faith-inspiring—it's fear-producing! I know I should be grateful to God, but things are tough right now. I just can't."

There is a discipline to seeing life with gratitude, even if you don't feel like it. Praise Him regardless. Praise and gratitude to God is a dynamic that will change your life. It is changing mine. As the late Catherine Marshall wrote in *Something More,* praising God in tough situations is like taking the negative things of life and plunging them into the positive solution of the presence of God, because the Lord inhabits the praises of His people.[4] Take your negatives and plunge them into praise. And in God's presence, Scripture says, is fullness of joy.

The story is told in Acts 16 of Paul and Silas being arrested, beaten, and thrown into a dungeon for preaching the Gospel. Their response? They began singing praises to God in the middle of the night in the dungeon. And a miracle happened—their chains fell off, and they were freed. I began to memorize Scriptures that directly spoke to fear and would carry them on small cards in my handbag, or I posted them on the refrigerator or put them in the car. I would sing Psalm 27: "The LORD is my light and my salvation; whom shall I fear?" "The angel of the LORD encamps all around those who fear Him" (Ps. 34:7). "Whenever I am afraid, I will trust in You" (Ps. 56:3). When I learned to focus on God's strength and power and praised Him—even in my anxieties—the fears began to go. Not instantly nor overnight, but they did leave.

LOOKING WITH LOVE

> *Love is a far better sustainer than fear.*
> *Fear enslaves, but love persuades.*[5]
>
> — FENELON

It can be tempting to look to another person to fill up all our holes, to make us complete. I was grateful for my husband and four sons, but I felt that somebody was missing in our family. I longed for my husband to know the love of a daughter, for my sons to have a sister—and especially for me to have a daughter! As we were unable to have more children, we explored adoption possibilities. Over time, we were approved by Holt Adoption Agency as parents for a three-year-old girl from South Korea.

Her little picture graced the front of the refrigerator as we waited the necessary two months for her to come home. We were given a shower with adorable little girl things—her bedroom was decorated and filled with stuffed animals. In 1984 on a rainy February afternoon, we found ourselves at a Northwest Orient gate in the Seattle airport, awaiting the arrival of our daughter—Kim Yung Ja, meaning "little one." We would call her Amy Kim Carmichael. Our hearts were pounding, and I could hardly wait to "pour myself" into my daughter. The daughter of my dreams would love pink frilly clothes (as I did), would love to read, love music, and love being with me. Of course. Finally she came off the plane, the last one off and half-asleep, carried in the arms of a volunteer.

We took Amy home, and I proceeded to "pour" myself into my daughter. Or tried to. As time went on, I realized Amy didn't like reading (we discovered she had very complex, puzzling learning disabilities). She also didn't like piano lessons. Instead, she likes crafts (I hate crafts) and baseball (I can't stand baseball). She didn't like dresses and preferred wearing jeans. We also found out that Amy's eyesight was very bad, and she needed to be fitted with special glasses. In addition, she had cavities in every tooth, and I was spending two or three afternoons a week in the office of a doctor, a speech therapist, or a dentist. Besides all that, she was unbelievably stubborn and could throw the most spectacular tantrums. I, a stoic Swede, could only stand and behold. I had never done tantrums. As time went on, I began to realize I was very frustrated and angry with Amy. Having her for a daughter was like getting a grocery cart with crooked wheels. And the harder I pushed, the more she resisted.

One day Amy blew up (I can't remember the issue) and screamed at me, "I hate you! I wish you were not my mother! Why did you adopt me anyway?" I tried to reason with her, but it was futile. She'd had it with me, deservedly so. I left her room and slowly walked downstairs, feeling devastated. *What have I done?* I wondered. *I've ruined her life and mine, too. God, what shall I do?*

In the middle of the stairs, a quiet thought came: *Have you thanked Me for her?* I had to admit I hadn't. "Lord," I prayed, "I can't seem to get through to her. I had expected something different. How can I mother her? I don't know how."

The order was gentle but definite: *Thank Me for her.*

Disappointment is a difficult emotion, but for one to move on from it, one must let go of certain expectations and be willing to see with fresh eyes. I had to back up emotionally and study her, really see her—not for what I needed her to be to me or for what I thought I wanted—but honestly see her. And then I began to thank God for Amy, appreciating what I had, not what I thought I'd wanted.

That began a definite turning point in our relationship. Let me tell you about my beautiful daughter Amy. A teenager now, she has a classic, beautiful style and looks terrific in red (pink is just not her color)! She has a wonderful tenacity and work ethic. She gets special help with her learning disabilities, but she works hard and competes in three sports a year—volleyball, basketball, and golf—besides playing the bass clarinet in the school band. And she has started to enjoy reading now that she has been fitted with specially made contact lenses. She is again trying her hand at the piano—now because she wants to—and has a gentle, artistic touch. She has a wonderful sense of humor and is compassionate toward kids who need help. Now that she is a sophomore in high school, she spends an hour a day helping with a first grade class. She has a spiritual depth that amazes me.

One day when she was in junior high, she came home and collapsed in sobs. Finally the story came out: Some older boys had been making her life miserable, teasing her, making fun of her speech and her ethnicity. After she calmed down, she told me, "Mom, when those boys kept teasing me, and I couldn't stand it, I just remembered Jesus on the cross when the people were mocking Him. He prayed, 'Father, forgive them for they know not what they do.' So I prayed that, too."

As I sat there and held her hand, I wondered who had the learning disabilities in our family. It certainly wasn't Amy. I am so grateful to God for her. Why? Because I finally saw her—and thanked God for her. I found out in a graphic way that when I thanked God for what He gave me—even if it wasn't what I thought I wanted—I was changed, and then God could work with my situation.

Not long ago our sons were discussing how many children they'd like to have, and they all agreed—they would like to adopt someday, too. I said another silent *Thank You, Lord.*

Amy says she has only one memory of the orphanage where she spent her early years. She says she remembers a long, dark hallway and looking out a small window. Why a window? Maybe she was longing for her mother, waiting for her to come back and get her. *Here I am, Amy. Thanks for the chance to be your mom!*

WINDOWS OF HOPE

> *For I know the thoughts that I think toward you, says the LORD, thoughts of peace and not of evil, to give you a future and a hope. Then you will call upon Me and go and pray to Me, and I will listen to you.*
>
> — JEREMIAH 29:11-12

Hope gets smothered sometimes when we feel trapped in a certain place or situation, and we wish we were back where we used to be or anyplace except where we are. But I'm learning it really isn't the circumstance as much as how I frame it, how I perceive it. When I look at a frustrating or negative situation through the window of hope and possibility—I am in an entirely new place. I've found that when I am in a place feeling stuck, it's often preparation for a new, wonderful place, but I'll never see it if I don't step back and look with eyes of hope.

Another word for hope is *expectation.* I love seeing the Three Sisters mountains near us, named by the early settlers Faith, Hope, and Charity. Not far from here, a party of explorers in the mid-1800s tried to find a way through the mountains and got hopelessly lost, not knowing where the pass was. Many in the party lost their lives that tragic winter.

Hope is like that mountain pass. It's the way *through* a dilemma, an impossible situation. We place our hope in God, expecting Him to provide an answer even though confusion surrounds us. With our eyes fixed on Him, we can hope, because He knows the way.

How does one keep one's hopes up when there seems to be no way, no clearly marked path? When it seems you're closed in? Psalm 32 talks about being surrounded by songs of deliverance and that He guides us with His eye.

"Lovingkindness in the morning . . . songs in the night . . . hope continually" (Ps. 42). That is what I live on when I am trying to get through. I identify with David, who said, "Why are you cast down, O my soul? And why are you disquieted within me? Hope in God; For I shall yet praise Him" (Ps. 43:5). Hope reminds me of realities I can't yet see—the reality that because I am His, God is at work in my life no matter how it seems, and I can move ahead with expectation. And when He is the object of my hope, I will never be disappointed.

Hope brings me to the place of being able to have faith in God. Hope encourages me to believe that He is involved in my life; He does care. What I may be seeing right now isn't the final story. Jesus said, "Lift up your eyes and look." He said, "Look up, for your redemption draws near." Proverbs says, "Without vision, the people perish."

> *Hope is the thing with feathers—That perches in the Soul—*
> *And sings the tune without the words—And never stops—at all.*[6]
>
> — EMILY DICKINSON

The morning sun streams in through tall wood-paneled windows in our dining room. The air is drenched with sunshine, the colors outside so crisp it's like a Van Gogh painting. Outside are Ponderosa pines, green grass, a row of aspen trees that Bill planted five summers ago, their golden tiny leaves shimmering in the morning light. The mountain air—cold at night, dry, yet fragrant with the scent of pine—fills my house.

As brilliantly as the sun shines through some days, there are many days that it does not shine at all. Some days the clouds cover the mountains, and I must remind myself they are still there. And so I must continually remember that it is God's love that perfects, that makes the windows of our lives clear, that helps us see. There's much we don't understand now. All the more reason to accept grace and praise Him exactly from where we are. As Scripture explains, "Now we see things imperfectly as in a poor mirror, but then we will see everything with perfect clarity. All that I know now is partial and incomplete, but then I will know everything completely, just as God knows me now. There are three things that will endure—faith, hope, and love—and the greatest of these is love" (1 Cor. 13:12-13 NLT).

THE WONDER OF WHAT YOU SEE

> *Be Thou my Vision, O Lord of my heart;*
> *Naught be all else to me save that Thou art.*[7]
>
> — MARY E. BYRNE

I love my home and where I live, but a couple of years ago I wanted to move away from here more than anything. Especially in the winter, this beautiful place can be very isolated. "I'm a people-person," I insisted to Bill. When the magazine publisher I worked for moved out of state and our sons began leaving home, I was ready to go, too. I wanted to move to Portland. I was ready to live in a city for a change. *How wonderful*, I thought, *to be near our grown-up children, to be near the airport, to be close to a church, shopping, and museums.* As much as I love the woods, sometimes I wish the trees could talk. But as we investigated the school situation for Amy, we realized she was doing very well where she was, and we needed to stay here for now. I was disappointed, to put it mildly.

"Another winter here, and I shall go mad," I promised myself. And then as I thought about it, God's still, small voice came to me: *What is it I have called you to do for now?* "Write books." *Can you think of a better place for you to do this?* I had to admit this place is God's provision for me now. Knowing me, if we lived nearer people, I would again be immersed up to my eyebrows in people and projects and not have the time to write. "Thank You, God," I had to say. It's amazing that I am content, but I am. And Amy is flourishing, which makes it worthwhile.

To see with eyes of wonder right where I am—really see it—puts me in a new place, although it may be the same old place. Daniel O'Leary tells the story of a boy who was fascinated by golden windows in the house on the hill. After supper the boy would look across the valley and wonder at the beauty that stirred him so deeply. One evening he made the long journey down in the dark valley and the dangerous climb up the rocky hill to the house with the windows of wonder. The perilous journey took him all night. Breathless with excitement, the boy collapsed wearily on the doorstep the next morning. "Is this the house with the golden windows?" he asked the woman at the door. She pointed back over the valley, and high on the hill was a little house, its windows on fire with the pure white light of the morning sun. "There," the woman gently said. "Where you live you will find the windows of wonder."[8]

WHAT'S YOUR PERSPECTIVE?

ఴ How can you live with a hope-filled attitude?

ఴ What difficult situation or person do you need to see with new eyes? To thank God for?

≪ For further study read Romans 5:1-11; 8:24-25; Hebrews 6:18-19.

≪

Lord, I pray against hopelessness and apathy that would crush dreams and choke out hope. I pray that I will open wide the windows of my soul to see that You want the best for my life. Help me notice the good things, Father. And fill all my vision with trust in You instead of fear. Give me faith to see opportunity even in impossible places. May I be so fully convinced of Your goodness that my life overflows with gratitude. In Jesus' name, amen.

≪

My Personal Reflections

_____

_____

_____

_____

_____

_____

_____

_____

_____

_____

_____

_____

Eight

❧

DOORS
IN MY HOUSE

❧

Lift up your heads, O you gates!
And be lifted up, you everlasting doors!
And the King of glory shall come in.

— PSALM 24:7

Bill designed the long, wide entrance to our front door with a series of graduated steps. With its bench-type railing, it's a wonderful place to catch the afternoon sun. In the summer I set out clay pots of flowers, strategically placing them away from deer who think it's their personal salad bar. The top half of our door is of leaded and beveled glass, and when the late afternoon sun comes through the glass, lovely prisms of color and designs flood the living room.

In nice weather I sit outside, usually sipping a cup of tea, soaking in the last bit of sun from the day while I listen to Chopin or some kind of sparkling music through my open door. For only a few fleeting moments the sun is just so.

I like to welcome guests at my front door, throwing the door open wide before they even have a chance to ring the bell, inviting them in with a smile and "Come on in!" The entrance of a house, they say, should reveal the owner's personality and set off the rest of the house. I would like to think my main entrance reflects my personality—welcoming, open.

But there are days when I don't want anyone to knock at my front door. To tell the truth, it's my back door—the one from the garage into the kitchen—that gets used most often. My back porch is usually a mess, with catchall shelves storing glass jars, sports equipment, basketball shoes whose owners have gone off and left them. There's a row of hooks where we hang our old jackets that we throw on before we go out for a walk. I'm embarrassed to have folks come into my house past this mess, but, to be honest, it's a truer reflection of me than my front door.

Although my front door is nice to see, it's not there just for looks—it's designed to let our guests know how to get in. Not long ago I stopped by to visit a new friend. Not having been to her house before, I sat in her driveway wondering which was the front door. There didn't seem to be a clearly defined entrance. After all, a door is powerful. It is the door that gives access to the house. Through it we invite others in or keep others out.

DOORS PROVIDE ACCESS

The soul's house—that interior dwelling place which we all possess, for the upkeep of which we are responsible—is a place in which we can meet God, or from which in a sense we can exclude God.[1]

—EVELYN UNDERHILL

Doors help define the purpose of the house. Walls within our house are necessary to give function and organization to various rooms, and the doors provide access to the house and to various rooms in the house. Imagine how useless a room would be without a door.

Yesterday I received an unexpected phone call from old friends. They were in the area and wondered if we could get together. Since

I have been working on this book for days, the house is dusty and needing a good cleaning. There are stacks of papers and books all over. I wanted them to come, no question. My heart knows they aren't coming to be served nor to see the condition of my house, even though I worry about it. They are coming to see our family, to reminisce and laugh about old times and talk about current challenges. So true friendship takes over, and I enthusiastically invite our very special friends. We have been through a lot together.

There are levels of relationship, of friendship. We have casual friendships. We have business and professional relationships. We have family relationships. And we have a few very close, intimate friends like the ones that just visited us who are welcome anytime. There's no such thing as an inconvenient visit. We are more honest with intimate friends; and over time, we grow to trust them.

Why Am I Reluctant to Open the Door?

Sometimes we resist opening the door to real friendship. It may be that we are afraid of being hurt. You may say, "I let somebody get close to me once, and I was deeply hurt. Never again—it isn't worth it." We may be afraid to get close to someone because we know we may be moving, and it would be another loss. We cannot bear the pain of caring and losing again, so we do not invest in friendships. Pain is a powerful motivator to keep us closed. If we open up to the truth in our lives, it may cause us pain to deal with it—so we avoid pain by staying closed, not letting anyone get too close.

We may be closed off to others by shame: "What do I have to give? He or she is so much more intelligent, wealthy, etc., than I am." Shame can isolate us and color how we view ourselves—as inferior, unworthy. Others get the message and avoid us.

Years ago when we were pastoring, a young woman my age in the church impulsively put her hand on my arm and offered sincerely, "If you ever need a friend or someone to talk to, please call me." I had admired her from a distance, but I had heard horror stories of confidences of pastor's wives being betrayed, so I said, "Thank you very much," adding inside, *That'll be the day.* I guarded my heart fiercely, and as a result, I was lonely.

But in spite of my reluctance, through the years I have been blessed to have friends who pursued friendship with me because they saw something they liked—and they trusted me with their hurts, their questions. I have learned that real friendship is a process of give and take—and that I in turn must "open the door" of my life to have real friends. Friendship is a two-way street, and for my friend to know me, I must be honest about my own feelings and struggles. It must be reciprocal. Yes, it is a risk, but so worth it. I am convinced that honest, trustworthy friends are some of the greatest blessings of life.

I have always struggled with loneliness, and yet loneliness is a reminder of my capacity for fellowship, for relationships that I must pursue. Loneliness is part of the human condition. Thomas Wolfe wrote, "The whole conviction of my life now rests upon the belief that loneliness, far from being a rare and curious phenomenon peculiar to myself and to a few other solitary men, is the central and inevitable fact of human existence."[2]

Perhaps loneliness is increased by the fast pace of our lives today or by our transience. Many of us live far from extended family and longtime friends. It is true that God has created us for relationship, and loneliness is a reminder to run into His presence, as He, too, longs for relationship with us. The poet James Weldon Johnson wrote:

> *And God stepped out on space,*
> *And He looked around and said:*
> *I'm lonely—*
> *I'll make me a world.*[3]

DOORS CAN PROVIDE PRIVACY

> *Come, my people, enter your chambers,*
> *And shut your doors behind you;*
> *Hide yourself, as it were, for a little moment.*
>
> — ISAIAH 26:20

It has been said that to be a friend to all is to be a friend to none. It is impossible to be intimate friends with everyone. Doors are symbolic of boundaries, necessary shields of protection. As time goes by, I am seeing how much I value privacy and solitude. Without it, I find it hard to give meaningfully. An acquaintance told a friend of mine that I did not ever let her see the real "me." My first reaction was to feel badly that she felt shut out of my life, but as I've thought about it, I realize I cannot be vulnerable with everyone. None of us can. Even Jesus poured Himself into twelve disciples—not the masses. Some people want access to rooms they have no business in.

Boundaries—closed doors—give our lives definition and are indicators of the unique persons God has created us to be, with unique giftedness. Some of us need more quiet time than others. He created us with personality needs, and each of us is wired differently. And yet the greatest commandment—to love God with all that we have and to love others—requires a willingness to be open, to be inconvenienced at times. We need discretion and an open heart to God for Him to show us the right balance in our relationships.

ROOMS SYMBOLIZE RELATIONSHIPS

> *He who can no longer listen to his brother will soon be no longer listening to God either; he will be doing nothing but prattle in the presence of God, too. Christians have forgotten that the ministry of listening has been committed to them by Him who is Himself the great listener and whose work they should share.*[4]
>
> — DIETRICH BONHOEFFER

Rooms symbolize relationships: We have relationship with ourselves, with friends, with colleagues, with neighbors. Some of the relationships that give us the most joy and the most pain are with family members. I recently saw a bumper sticker: "All men are idiots, and I married their king!" Within the family we learn very early how to push each other's buttons. If you have children, you know what I mean.

When our second son Eric was three years old, he had an imaginary friend named "Charlie Beakey," who was always very nice to him. Charlie would play any game Eric wanted and was always with him, always listened to him. Too bad he was imaginary, because he was an ideal friend. How incredibly important it is to feel heard within the family unit and, unfortunately, how rare. Too often we take one another within the family for granted. We see each other as commodities to be used—objects—rather than precious, unique people.

Do you have someone in your family, maybe in the distant past, maybe in your life now, who listens to you? Somehow when you're with this person, you feel most fully yourself, because he or she sees you. You feel visible, more alive, just by being with this person. I was blessed to have a mother who really listened to me. Once in a while she would catch us up with a hug and a smile and ask, "What does it feel like to be you?" And she really wanted to know. Most days it's easy just to let the sounds of my family's voices wash over me. I hear them, but if I truly listen, I must get involved. It takes work and attention to listen to what is being said as well as to what is not being said, to read body language. It takes courage at times to respond to the emotion behind the words, not just to the words.

Listening to someone may be the most effective way to say to that person, "I love you." Jesus said, "Greater love has no man than this, that a man lay down his life for his friends." *Listening* can certainly be a way to "lay down our lives," because it means to lay aside my own desire to be heard, to wait before forming an opinion. First John

3:17 says, "But whoever has this world's goods, and sees his brother in need, and shuts up his heart from him, how does the love of God abide in him?" We can "shut up" our hearts to those closest to us by not taking the time to get out of ourselves and see and hear them.

Of course, we can't listen intently all the time. That would be exhausting. But so much of the time we carry on conversations, and our words sail right past each other. Two simple qualities greatly improve relationships within families—respect for the other and cultivating the art of listening. If we care enough to listen, we are showing respect. Respect is simply extending common courtesy. Respect for another—especially one with whom we are very familiar—means to respect his or her privacy, not barging through doors, literally or figuratively. It means not prying, waiting if necessary to be invited in. "Love is . . . not rude" (1 Cor. 13:4–5 NLT).

Letting God into All the Rooms

> *O Lord, the house of my soul is narrow;*
> *enlarge it that you may enter in. It is ruined.*
> *O repair it! It displeases your sight; I confess it, I know.*
> *But who shall cleanse it, or to whom shall I cry but you?*
> *Cleanse me from secret faults, O Lord, and spare*
> *your servant from strange sins.*[5]
>
> —AUGUSTINE

"Perfect love," 1 John 4:18 says, "casts out fear." The one who will never leave me, never forsake me, is the one who stands outside the door of my heart, knocking, waiting for me to invite Him in. "Behold, I stand at the door and knock," He says. "If anyone hears My voice and opens the door, I will come in to him and dine with him, and he with Me" (Rev. 3:20).

Holman Hunt's famous painting of Christ standing outside

knocking at a door is displayed at St. Paul's Cathedral in London. Below the painting is a description: "On the left-hand side of the picture is seen this door of the human soul. It is fast barred; its bars and nails are rusty; it is knitted and bound to its stanchions by creeping tendrils of ivy, showing that it has never been opened."[6]

This painting is an eloquent description of God's pursuit of us, His children. Sometimes we respond to Him, and sometimes we do not. Regardless, He waits for the invitation. He will not intrude. The third chapter of Revelation is a fascinating study on some very important doors, metaphorically speaking. There is a message given to two churches from the Lord—one to the church at Philadelphia and one to the Laodicean church. To the Philadelphia church—where people really knew how to love one another—the Lord said, "This is the message from the one who is holy and true. He is the one who has the key of David. He opens doors, and no one can shut them; he shuts doors, and no one can open them" (Rev. 3:7 NLT). Later on in the letter to the Laodicean church, Jesus warns them for being lukewarm. This is the context of the wonderful message from our Lord: "Behold I stand at the door and knock." What is the implication? That to know and live in God's love means He places before us an open door. And to the self-satisfied and complacent, Jesus says, "Behold I stand at your door and knock." What great love that He will pursue us, even in our ignorance and pride, wanting to come in and restore us even in our self-sufficiency.

Once when I was very small, my mother told us children for our bedtime story the "old, old story" of Jesus dying for our sins. I remember lying in bed in the darkened room, tears streaming down my face as it seemed I heard for the first time the story of the Cross. I cried silently, not wanting my brothers or sisters to hear me. I was deeply moved even at that tender age by the story of redemption. When Mother finished telling the story, she sang as a lullaby, "Into my heart, into my heart, come into my heart, Lord Jesus. Come in today; Come in to stay. Come into my heart, Lord Jesus." I knew instinctively even then that I needed cleansing inside—that it was the only solution for guilt. The power of that simple story still moves me, although I do not really understand it. I only know that because Christ died on the cross, I can say without fear, "Come in," to God.

Even though my house is broken and dirty in places and in such need of cleansing, He becomes the door for me to God—my wholeness, my cleansing—if I simply believe and invite Him in. Jesus said, "I am the door. If anyone enters by Me, he will be saved" (John 10:9). Inviting Him in is not a one-time event. He must be at home in our lives. My dearest and most intimate friends have been at my house frequently and feel at home there. They don't ask where my bathroom is or if they can get a drink of water. They're familiar with my house. They can take their shoes off, relax.

I want God to be so at home with me that He knows He is welcome anytime, that He has access to all of the rooms in my house. All of them. Paul said in Ephesians 3:17-19, "And I pray that Christ will be more and more at home in your hearts as you trust in him. May your roots go down deep into the soil of God's marvelous love. And may you have the power to understand, as all God's people should, how wide, how long, how high, and how deep his love really is. May you experience the love of Christ, though it is so great you will never fully understand it. Then you will be filled with the fullness of life and power that comes from God" (NLT).

Imagine: To be in relationship with the sovereign God of this universe, our Creator. It is astonishing to think that He can be a close friend, closer than a brother. And it may be a volatile relationship, perhaps distant. It is, after all, a relationship. "I'll only go so far with You, God." "I'm not sure I trust You." Or, "Let's talk. I'd like get to know You more."

C. S. Lewis wrote, "I willingly believe that the damned are, in one sense, successful, rebels to the end; that the doors of hell are locked on the inside."[7] My reluctance to open my heart's door to Him can mirror my attitude toward others. I may just not want to be bothered, or I am busy with my own agenda. Maybe I'm reluctant to let Him inside because my house is dirty, and I don't feel acceptable.

More than anybody, I know where the dirt is in my house. And no matter how clean the rest of my house is, if my bathrooms and laundry room are dirty, my house feels dirty. But inside my house, in my closet, in my private room, there is no public face.

Possibly the most important relationship you have (other than with God) is with yourself. Honesty is the first step. It can be scary to take a good, hard look at oneself. But if I enter this innermost chamber, daring to see the truth about myself with my hand in His, knowing He loves me, it is liberating. Jesus said, "You will know the truth, and the truth will set you free" (John 8:32 NIV).

Truth—as painful and uncomfortable as it is—liberates. Why? Because when we see the truth about ourselves, we see our need for forgiveness and healing. And then we can truly grow. In his small but profound little book *The Wounded Healer*, Henri Nouwen wrote,

> How can we [offer creative ways to others to know Him]? . . . I think by no other way than to enter ourselves first of all into the center of our existence and become familiar with the complexities of our inner lives. As soon as we feel at home in our own house, discover the dark corners as well as the light spots, the closed doors as well as the draft rooms, our confusion will evaporate, our anxiety will diminish, and we will become capable of creative work.[8]

The Door to the Secret Place

"Oh, taste and see that the Lord is good" (Ps. 34:8). Find a period every day for reading, meditation and prayer. This will become easy

when you truly love Him. We never wonder what we will talk about.
He is our friend. Our hearts are open to Him. We must be completely
candid with Him, holding nothing back. Even if there is nothing we
care to say to Him, it is a joy just to be in His presence.[9]

— FENELON

Within my house, I have special places, some more private than others. Our bedrooms of course are private, and then there are rooms that we share, such as the kitchen, dining room, and family room. I have a small study in which I can shut the door and be alone, surrounded by books.

When I was a girl, I often had a secret place. Sometimes my secret place was in the hayloft of the big old barn. If a granary was empty, it made a great secret place. I can still see in my mind's eye the shafts of light streaming in from the high windows of the granary as I swung on the iron bars that crisscrossed the inside of the room. I could bolt the door from the inside, and no one could get in without my permission. When my little brothers or sisters discovered my place, I had to find a new one. It had to be my place, and mine alone. Sometimes I just wanted to be quiet and listen to the doves in the rafters of the barn, or if I was outside, to feel the wind on my face and see the swallows wheeling against the sky.

After I grew up and left the farm, I didn't seek out a secret place so much anymore, and the secret place gradually became a distant childhood memory. As life changed for me, and my family increased and life grew more complex, I realized I was missing my secret place, the place where God and I could be alone. There were so many things I needed to pour out before Him.

In the Hebrew, the word for secret place is *sether*, meaning a covering, a hiding place.[10] How do we find these places? The main requirement is solitude—a place to be alone. This is not easy when

you have a life like mine! I have to look for the secret place, a place
to go in, to shut the door behind me. This takes some ingenuity and
flexibility sometimes. I remember reading that Susannah Wesley,
with her many children and responsibilities, put her apron over her
head for an hour and shut herself in with God.

I identify with both Mary and Martha, Jesus' friends (Luke 10).
Martha was the one preparing the meal and working so hard for the
Lord; on the other hand, Mary sat at Jesus' feet listening to Him,
which Jesus said was the "necessary part." Part of me sympathizes
with Martha, too, because, let's face it, without the Marthas in life,
nobody would be fed!

Although time alone with God is essential, we don't have to live
a cloistered life in order to pray. Prayer can be a natural part of living. Phillips Brooks said, "A prayer in its simplest definition is
merely a wish turned Godward." If you're uncomfortable praying in
front of others, you're in good company. Jesus said the man who
stood on the street corner praying eloquently, loudly, and publicly
was not praying nearly as effectively as the man who simply and privately prayed, "Lord, be merciful to me, a sinner."

Don't ever be ashamed for feeling awkward or for giving short,
humble prayers. What is prayer anyway? It's not for the benefit of
others in the room. If honesty is a requirement for a good human
relationship, how much more is honesty important with God. Our
prayers must be honest. God knows our hearts anyway, so we can
pray from who we are. Jesus said in Matthew 6:5-6:

> *And when you pray, you shall not be like the hypocrites. For they love
> to pray standing in the synagogues and on the corners of the streets,
> that they may be seen by men. Assuredly, I say to you, they have their
> reward. But you, when you pray, go into your room, and when you
> have shut your door, pray to your Father who is in the secret place; and
> your Father who sees in secret will reward you openly.*

Why is the work of prayer so essential these days? I believe it is because the real battles that are being waged are spiritual ones. If Christ indeed is at home in our lives, we can access His power for the needs in our lives and in the lives of our families and friends. Yes, we have great needs—but more than that, we have a great Savior who really listens to us, who actually came down to earth to take on human form so that He would know "what it feels like to be you." And the book of Hebrews says He is touched by the feeling of our infirmities (4:15 KJV).

Knowing of His great love for each of us, how can we not want such a one to come into our lives? He says, "My beloved . . . come away. . . . Let me see your face; let me hear your voice" (Song of Solomon 2:10-14). You may have a special "prayer closet" in your house, but my places change, depending on what's going on in my life. I have to find new places, just as I did when I was a girl.

I go into my bedroom and close the door or close the door of my study. I go for a walk, knowing "God, You are ever with me." Or while driving down the street, I turn the radio off and tune in to His presence. Our circumstances are different, presenting their own challenges to getting alone with God.

The inner chamber of prayer is not just a physical place; it is a spiritual place, an attitude. As I look back on the many places where God has met me in my life, it was in the places of loss and disillusionment and disappointment where it seemed God was saying, "Meet Me here!" If you feel turned inside out and helpless against life, you are in a great place to allow Jesus into that very place to begin a great work deep within you.

Henri Nouwen writes, "He is the source of all peace. Where is this peace to be found? In our own weakness, in those places where we feel most broken, most insecure, most in agony, most afraid."[11]

The Waiting Room

> *I waited patiently for the LORD, and He inclined to me.*
>
> — PSALM 40:1

The "waiting room" of prayer is one some of us would like to skip. We want answers now, results now. But God is not on our timetable; we must be on His. That is what it means to wait on God, to be in His presence, understanding His purposes for the situations that I'm concerned about.

When I finally find my time to wait on Him, I lay before Him my "top ten" list. Sometimes it's longer, sometimes it's shorter, and sometimes it's more vague. Sometimes it's not so much a list as a longing. And then through prayer I invite Him in—into me. Into my "inner chamber" that Saint Teresa of Avila described nearly five hundred years ago. But my inner room is often crowded, cluttered, like the back porch through the laundry room. Some things dominate this inner chamber—on my mind so much that there's hardly room for Him to get in. "Lord," I plead, "fix this. Change this. Please! God, this situation is not good, don't You see? It can't be Your will!"

But God through Scripture says to me, "Seek My face," and I respond, "Your face, Lord, I will seek" (Ps. 27). And so I wait. Isaiah 40:31(KJV) says, "They that wait upon the Lord shall renew their strength."

In the silence of waiting, a gentle understanding comes to me of what waiting means. I gradually let go of the things in my inner life—the very things, the very people I have been holding up to God. I let them go—into His hands, His care, knowing He hears me. And I wait, aware of His presence. Wait. Psalm 40:1 says, "I waited patiently for the LORD, and He inclined to me."

It has always been difficult for us humans to be still before God. John Donne preached in 1626, "I throw myself down in my chamber, and I call in and invite God and his angels thither, and when they are there, I neglect God and his angels, for the noise of a fly, for the rattling of a coach, for the whining of a door."[12]

The psalmist wrote, "My eyes are ever toward the LORD" (25:15). My eyes are ever toward the Lord—not the problem, not the need. And in this waiting, I see that prayer is simply being with almighty God, resting in His strength. And time alone in the prayer closet has an effect on the rest of our lives—the rest of our rooms.

CONSIDER THE DOORS IN YOUR LIFE

∾ Do I need to protect my "inner life" with God by cultivating a secret place?

∾ Am I open to healthy, real friendships?

∾ Do I "invite" others into my life?

∾ Who is the first person who really understood me? What did he or she do for me? How can I be this person to someone else?

∾ Is God at home in my entire house, my entire life? Does He have access to every room in my life, every closet?

∾ For further study read James 1:19; 1 John 3:16; Revelation 3; 1 John 3:17-23.

∾

Lord, You know my innermost heart and my deepest agonies, my secret dreams. I long to be used wholly for You, to live a focused life of purpose, of love and goodness. But life trips me up, Lord. Often I am selfish, and don't want to open up to other people. I can be too busy to take time to wait on You. But thank You for Your mercy and love that makes it possible for me to have relationship with You.

May I hear Your gentle knock on my heart's door always. And may I respond with love and joy to You, "Come in!" Teach me how to truly love others for Your name's sake. Amen.

જી

My Personal Reflections

_____

_____

_____

_____

_____

_____

_____

_____

_____

_____

_____

_____

_____

_____

_____

_____

_____

_____

_____

_____

_____

Nine

❧

DECORATING

❧

Through wisdom a house is built,
And by understanding it is established;
By knowledge the rooms are filled
With all precious and pleasant riches.

— PROVERBS 24:3-4

The other day I came home from an overnight trip and tried to look with new eyes at my house, as a visitor would see it. It seems to me that our house is comfortable and casual, unmistakably a family house, the kind of place where you don't think twice about putting your feet up on the ottoman. When I have company, I try valiantly to polish furniture and straighten things, but *functional* is definitely the key word here. Most of the furnishings in our house are ordinary couches, end tables, and lamps—practical and well used.

There are lots of bookshelves crammed full of books—some of them old friends I can't bear to throw away, like my worn, often-read copy of *How Green Was My Valley*. I love to read it occasionally just for the music of the Welsh language.

Our most pressing need right now is our bed situation. The twin bunk beds up in the boys' dorm room don't fit our boys who are now all over six feet tall. I keep threatening to move the bunks, but I have it in the back of my mind that if we can keep this house long enough, grandchildren may fit them.

My favorite item in the house is a baby grand piano that Bill bought for me from a family who wanted to get a pool table instead. We finally got the piano moved up to the loft over the living room after gouging a huge hole in the wall of the stairway. Bill says the piano will go with the house when we sell, because there's no way we can ever get it out of there. I also cherish our large oak dining room table and chairs that easily seat twelve. It's big, solid, and glows with memories we've had around the table with friends and family, with promise of more to come. In fact, there's a scorched place on the surface where a candle burned too long at Christmas one year.

Decorations and furnishings exist to meet the common human needs of the inhabitants of the house—hunger, weariness, loneliness, and discouragement. Upon these very ordinary items on which we rest (beds), converse (couches and chairs), and eat (tables and chairs, kitchen utensils, etc.), we live our lives and offer what we have to those who visit. The beauty, creativity, and meaning we apply to these mundane articles bring delight, comfort, and pleasure. The furnishings also give personality and unique style to your house.

Clare Cooper Marcus, professor of architecture at UC Berkeley, recently published results of twenty years of research in *House as a Mirror of Self.*[1] She asserts that one's house reflects one's self. If that indeed is true, my clutter tells a lot about me. I take too much in and hang onto it as long as possible. I have a sweater hanging in my closet that I wore home from the hospital when Jon was born twenty-seven years ago. (The kids tell me it's back in style now though!)

What is in your house? Houses on the same street may appear similar; yet the inside is unique, as we all have our individual quirks. When my sister Kitty gets in my kitchen, she complains that she can never find the utensils she needs. Of course, she has everything in her kitchen. Her kitchen is color-coordinated and equipped with the latest gadgets. She is an excellent cook and can prepare a gourmet meal for 200 at the drop of a hat. I'm still using the same stuff in my kitchen that I got at my wedding shower thirty years ago. But I have hundreds of books!

> If you want a golden rule that will fit everybody, this is it: Have nothing in your house that you do not know to be useful, or believe to be beautiful.
>
> *— THE BEAUTY OF LIFE* [2]

TWO WOMEN, TWO INTERIORS

Second Kings chapter four tells the stories of two women who had very different furnishings within their houses. Yet each saw God meet them where they were.

The first woman was a young widow of the son of a prophet (vs. 1-7). She made no effort to hide her desperation. Her house was in big trouble. Her husband had died, and the bill collectors were coming to take her sons into slavery to pay for the outstanding debts. She was emotionally destitute, suffering from her great loss. And she was a single parent, worried about her sons. She had no money, no food.

She went to the prophet under whom her husband was studying and told him, "Your servant my husband is dead, and you know that your servant feared the LORD. And the creditor is coming to take my two sons to be his slaves" (v. 1).

Elisha asked her, "What shall I do for you? Tell me, what do you have in the house?"

And she said, "Nothing . . . but a jar of oil."

God always deals with us right where we are, with what we have. It was Mother Teresa who said, "What wonders God has done with nothingness!" (Don't be afraid of your "nothing" answers—this is a creative place to be.)

Elisha told her, "Go, borrow vessels from everywhere, from all your neighbors—empty vessels; do not gather just a few . . . . Pour it into all those vessels." As she poured the oil, it miraculously kept coming until all the vessels were filled. She sold the oil and got out of debt (vv. 3-7).

At first glance the other woman described in this same chapter, known as the Shunammite woman, would seem not to have much in common with the young widow. She seemed to have everything the destitute widow did not—wealth, political influence, talent, resources, confidence, a husband who provided well for her. She was a giver and was known for her hospitality, perhaps the Martha Stewart of her day. She not only provided meals for Elisha and his servant Gehazi, but she also had her husband build an apartment for Elisha and considerately furnished it with a bed, a table and chair, and a lamp. Life didn't exempt her from disappointment though. Gehazi noticed: "She has no son, and her husband is old."

Elisha gave her a word from God: "This time next year you shall embrace a son." Money and influence can't buy some things. She was as desperate as the widow; it just wasn't as obvious. In five short verses, we see God answering her heart's desire: She had a son; he grew. Then one tragic day, the boy came in from the field where he'd been with his father, sat on his mother's lap, and died, perhaps of a heat stroke.

She laid the boy on Elisha's bed and hurried to Mt. Carmel where Elisha and Gehazi were. Elisha saw her in the distance and told his servant to run to meet her and ask, "Is it well with you? Is it well with your husband? Is it well with the child?" Something had to be terribly wrong for her to seek him out.

Her answer: "All is well." (Really?) She went on to say, "Did I ask a son of my lord? Did I not say, 'Do not deceive me'?" In other words,

"Don't play games with me. Don't give me something wonderful and then tear it away from me." This talented, gifted woman—the one everyone else relied on—was now devastated. When Elisha got to where the boy was, he went in, shut the door behind him, and touched the child in faith. And the child lived and was restored to his mother (vv. 8-37).

From these two different women whose houses had very different interiors, I learn these principles:

God knows what is inside my house, my unique personality and place in life. He knows my obvious needs and the ones that may not be obvious.

God can meet the needs within my house, regardless of what they are.

The person doesn't exist who doesn't have a need inside his or her house, and I must not compare my house with the house down the street. I don't know—really—what is inside that house.

I can give delight, pleasures out of the gifts He gives me.

One spring morning outside the dining room window, I saw two nuthatches building a nest in the birdhouse hanging from a nearby tree. They worked together, taking turns bringing in twigs and straw to build a safe and warm place for their young. It is just programmed into them by the Creator to do this; and it is something we do, too, put in us by our Creator, furnishing and decorating our homes for the ones we love. Maybe it's practicing for the real thing. After all, Jesus left to prepare dwelling places for us in the Father's house where someday we'll be together.

Regardless of our personality, style, or unique giftedness, there are some basic "furnishings" God wants us to have. These six important concepts describe what's in the Father's house. We can have these qualities, too.

1. *Do I offer a place of rest?*

Come to Me, all you who labor and are heavy laden, and I will give you rest. Take My yoke upon you and learn from Me, for I am gentle and lowly in heart, and you will find rest for your souls.

—MATTHEW 11:28-29

Now that I travel more than I used to, I realize anew as I snuggle under my comforter that there is nothing like my own bed! Part of what relaxes me so is knowing this is my own place, and I am safe here. I don't have to impress anyone with brilliant conversation or worry about my hair. It is a place to relax, to be near the ones I love the most. Do others feel safe with me? Have I learned what it means to keep confidences and allow others to be vulnerable?

Do I know what it means to enter into His rest, as the writer to the Hebrews described (Hebrews 4)? Understanding what Sabbath means is important—our Creator knows our complexities, that we need times of rest and renewal. I have much to learn about this. Amy said to me the other day, "Mom, stop working so much. Just sit down with me." When I am relaxed, others around me will feel free to relax, too.

2. *Do I offer a place of nourishment?*

He brought me to the banqueting house, and his banner over me was love.

—SONG OF SOLOMON 2:4

The kitchen is the heart of the home, the place where we offer food and drink that nourishes us for the journey ahead, restores to us energy we've expended. It's heartwarming to walk into a home filled with the fragrance of a savory stew simmering or bread baking and to see a table set with a candle burning. It says, "This is for you because

I care about your most basic needs. I have been planning for you to come because you are loved and wanted here." These mundane acts of service can be profound statements of love and acceptance.

God's Word nourishes me, gives me courage to go on. He knows me and welcomes me to His table. It is by being nourished by His Word that I can give out to others. As the prophet Jeremiah wrote, "Your words were found, and I ate them, and Your word was to me the joy and rejoicing of my heart; For I am called by Your name, O LORD God of hosts" (15:16). He is wonderfully accessible to me in common, ordinary life, as He has been to all who have sought Him throughout the ages.

Hundreds of years ago, Brother Lawrence wrote, "Lift up your heart to Him, sometimes even at your meals, and when you are in company; the least little remembrance will always be acceptable to Him. You need not cry very loud; He is nearer to us than we are aware of."[3] We can nourish others by our unique creativity and gifts.

3. Do I offer a place of peace?

Peace I leave with you, My peace I give to you; not as the world gives do I give to you. Let not your heart be troubled, neither let it be afraid.

— JOHN 14:27

Peace means there is order, harmony. The colors are pleasing and coordinated, thoughtfully planned. Furnishings, by their design and arrangement, can subtly promote a sense of peace or jarring confusion. Shortly after we were married, I decided to put wallpaper in my bathroom to perk it up a bit. I chose a black and white geometric design, but I didn't get it on straight. Also water left streaks on the paper that I never could get out. Every time I went into that bathroom, I cringed. It was not harmonious nor pleasing to the eye. At least people didn't linger in the bathroom long!

But peace is much more than design, color, or furniture; real peace comes from deep within. When I was a guest speaker in one city, I stayed in a beautiful home. It was decorated flawlessly, with every personal consideration anticipated. And yet from the moment I walked in the door, I sensed strife, unease in the home. It was only later after I spoke at length with my hostess that I learned that the family was embroiled in a difficult, tense situation that involved each of them in different ways. There was no peace.

Life is full of cares, and it's easy to lose peace. Not long ago I was rushing through my morning devotions, and my Bible reading for that morning was Mark 4:36-41. I was distracted as I read, worrying about various things regarding the children and about my deadline. Suddenly I became aware of what I was reading: Jesus was asleep in the boat in the midst of a storm, and His disciples were terrified that they would sink. They awoke Jesus, and He stood, calmed the storm, and rebuked the disciples for their little faith. I realized that I, too, was all "churned up" inside—thinking Jesus must surely be asleep in my "house," and all would be lost. I prayed, "Jesus, forgive me for not believing! You are in my home, my family. Speak Your peace to my storms. Amen." There is peace because the Lord is there, and He has authority—I simply must have faith to believe Him.

I've visited homes where I was made to feel comfortable, welcomed. And there are homes where I've felt that my visit was an intrusion, an inconvenience. What makes a home a shelter rather than a prison? It is an atmosphere of safety, peace, and love. To become a "house for God"—a place where love dwells—means welcoming people and experiences that God sends my way. That is not always easy for me. And yet I have seen that it is often in the interruptions or intrusions that real life happens.

4. Do I offer a place of authentic fellowship?

I thank my God upon every remembrance of you . . . for your
fellowship in the gospel from the first day until now.

— PHILIPPIANS 1:3, 5

Many years ago when we were youth pastors, we were leaving the church where we'd been employed. It was not a happy departure as it was not our choice to leave. We'd just been part time while Bill was in graduate school, and they wanted to hire a full-time youth pastor. I was pregnant, so as a farewell, the church gave us a baby shower on a Sunday afternoon.

Someone had nicely decorated a cake as the centerpiece for the table. After we opened the gifts, the hostess whisked the cake away to the kitchen and brought out some cookies. She explained that the cake wasn't real; it was just a pan turned upside down and decorated. She took the pan into the church kitchen and washed it off before she took it home.

Why does this memory—so long buried—still sting? I think it's because the phony cake symbolized what was actually going on— pseudo-fellowship. There was a sense of unreality about the whole afternoon, the river of emotions beneath the surface unacknowledged.

But I have offered the same pseudo-fellowship, at times asking a friend, "How are you?" and not really wanting to know. Or I replied brightly with my own "I'm doing great—thanks," when inside I am dying. When we are not real, we deny one another true fellowship. Why do I spend so much effort covering up the real me? Maybe it's because I know at heart that I am not good enough. Like you, I'm weak, sinful, inadequate, and I know I will inevitably disappoint someone. I fear abandonment and rejection. And so we present something decorated beautifully that looks like fellowship but isn't. It's hollow and phony because it isn't real.

It is one thing to have a wonderfully decorated and furnished house; but is the house for you, or do you exist for the house? We have real fellowship when we feel safe with one other, when there is earned trust in the relationship. Fellowship is for us, for real people with real needs. There is nothing sweeter than authentic relationships. The psalmist wrote, "Behold, how good and how pleasant it is for brethren to dwell together in unity!" (Ps. 133:1).

5. *Do I offer a place of comfort?*

I will fear no evil; for You are with me; Your rod and Your staff, they comfort me.

—PSALM 23:4

When children are young, their senses are keen, and they are sensitive to strange environments. Think back to when you were very small and experienced your first sleepover or a night somewhere different. You noticed things—the textures in the blankets, the carpeting, the smells, the pictures on the wall. You were sharply aware of your friends' parents or the adults in charge who were not your parents, and it was an alien environment to you. Perhaps you got homesick; or if you are adventurous, it was fun for you.

When I was very small, I tended to get homesick when I was away from my parents. I vividly remember coming back from staying with a friend so homesick I was physically ill. As soon as I got home, the ache inside of me subsided. I was immediately comforted by being in the presence of those I loved. It was healing to touch them, to hear their voices, to be near.

Often the world feels alien, strange; and the people "in charge" are unrighteous, and I just feel homesick. Jesus promised us that He would return, and we would someday all be together. Meanwhile, He sent us the Comforter, the Holy Spirit, and we can comfort one another with this hope:

> *For the Lord Himself will descend from heaven with a shout, with the voice of an archangel, and with the trumpet of God. And the dead in Christ will rise first. Then we who are alive and remain shall be caught up together with them in the clouds to meet the Lord in the air. And thus we shall always be with the Lord. Therefore comfort one another with these words.*
>
> —1 THESSALONIANS 4:16-18

5. *Do I offer a place of delight, pleasure?*

> *Delight yourself also in the LORD, and He shall give you the desires of your heart.*
>
> —PSALM 37:4

It is the little things that delight me so in my house—flowers that I finally coax to bloom, the gleam of clean glass, the shine of polished wood. The mirrors in the entry add an illusion of light and space. In the summer windows on the opposite wall overlook trees and grass and my hanging baskets of flowers. In the winter often there is a fire burning in the fireplace, giving off warmth. Even the quiet company of our cat, who considers it an art form to find the best splashes of sunlight to nap in, adds pleasure.

Recently forest fires were burning too near our home, and we had to consider what we would take if we were evacuated. People, of course, first. But for actual things—the really important things that we could not replace—we would choose family pictures, the children's baby books, letters, the old family Bible that came from Sweden with my grandparents, scrapbooks. Maybe the Blue Calico tea set that Bill and I got in England and some precious things from our parents. These personal touches remind us of people, of places, and they delight and pleasure us.

> *The LORD is my shepherd; I shall not want. . . . You prepare a table before me in the presence of my enemies.*
>
> — PSALM 23:1, 5

Different rooms in your house take on different functions depending on what's going on with you right now. So it is with my life. Now that I spend much time in writing and speaking, my life is different from what it used to be, and I must give myself permission to be flexible with my house and delight myself in God where I am today.

I am trying to understand a lesson from nature—to learn to delight in the rhythm of the seasons of my life and remember that "there is a time for everything, a season for every activity under heaven" (Eccl. 3:1 NLT). Henri Nouwen wrote:

> The mystery of life is that the Lord of life cannot be known except in and through the act of living. Without the concrete and specific involvements of daily life, we cannot come to know the loving presence of Him who holds us in the palm of His hand. Our limited acts of love reveal to us His unlimited love. Our small gestures of care reveal His boundless care. Our fearful and hesitant words reveal His fearless and guiding Word. It is indeed through our broken, vulnerable, mortal ways of being that the healing power of the eternal God becomes visible to us. Therefore, we are called each day to present to our Lord the whole of our lives.[4]

A SIMPLE HOUSE

> *And what does the LORD require of you but to do justly, to love mercy, and to walk humbly with your God?*
>
> — MICAH 6:8

A simple, honest home is the best, I secretly believe. A place where you don't need much—just the basics of shelter, warmth. A place to rest. Simplicity is difficult to achieve, as a good interior decorator will tell you. It's easy to over-design, over-accessorize. Elegance is more often achieved by what you leave out. Limits of time and money are actually liberating, as it helps creativity.

There is a little cabin that somehow in my mind will always be a piece of home to me. Although events and circumstances have changed and many loved ones are gone now that made it our special place, when I think of it, I can still hear the distant rushing river below and smell the fragrant pines that surrounded the cabin.

Several years ago we were vacationing with our children at this place near Glacier Park that has been in our family for years. This two-room cabin nestles under tall pine trees and is rustic, heated only by a woodstove. There's no indoor plumbing, but the cabin is charming anyway, the inside covered with knotty pine and memories.

Our children, under the direction of our oldest son Jon, then thirteen, informed Bill and me they were going to fix us a special anniversary meal. That evening they sat us down to the most memorable feast I have ever had. On the menu was rainbow trout, caught that day in the river near the cabin, and corn on the cob wrapped in foil and roasted on the outside grill with the trout. For dessert we had ice cream with fresh huckleberries. Our "waiters" and "chefs" wore rumpled blue jeans and T-shirts and served dinner to us on the same wobbly table covered with the same checkered oilcloth that has been there since I was a little girl. The centerpiece was a blue jug filled with daisies we'd picked outside the cabin.

"Where did you get the huckleberries?" Bill asked, amazed.

They told us they'd pooled their money and bought the dinner ingredients at a little store (except for the fish, which they caught themselves). "We ran out of money, and the man at the store let us have the rest free," they told us.

What made it so memorable? Real love. The meal itself was simple, yet wonderful. Our children gave everything they had to put that meal together, and even though they didn't have enough, it became enough.

In John 6 Jesus had been preaching to the multitudes (vv. 1-14). There were thousands of hungry people, and they were far from anywhere to get food. The only food to be found was a small boy's lunch of five barley loaves and two fish. The boy was willing to offer what he had though, and as Andrew brought it to Jesus, he asked skeptically, "What's this, with so many?" But as Jesus blessed and broke the humble lunch, it miraculously multiplied to feed them all.

I've often felt like Andrew. How can my one ordinary life with all its frailties and imperfections feed anybody? I tend to want "more" in my house—I want to be sure I have what I need, so my tendency is to gather more into my house, my life. But I'm discovering that willingness from a simple heart is the important thing—to present my offerings as a child, not being complicated and guarded, even though it may be humble fare. And at His miraculous touch, it can nourish and sustain others.

The Important Is Often Mundane

I've learned that often the most important things in our lives are not on the calendar. Instead, they often come through ordinary days. An interruption. An unexpected visitor. An inconvenience. A surprise. We make elaborate plans and schemes; then real life intrudes. This is the improvising, the wonderful creativity that makes a house—and a life—livable, approachable. Somehow it's the ordinary, the week days, the chronic chores, the laundry, the suppers, the same relationships that require the most of us. As the poet described, we are "magnificently unprepared for the long littleness of life."[5]

It was Sunday, and we were on our way home from church. It had been a hectic week as we were involved in a major remodeling of our house. In between everything else Bill and I were doing, we tried to do at least one project a day on the house as we were eager to get through with the mess. This particular afternoon (even though I felt vaguely guilty doing it on Sunday), I had quietly resolved to paint the railing in the family room. I'd botched it up with the wrong paint, but now I had the right paint, and I could get that job crossed off the list.

Chris broke into my thoughts. "Mom, see those bluffs over there? I've heard that's a great hike. Let's pack our lunches and go up there."

"Well, I was going to paint, but . . . " The eager look on his face weakened my resolve. "All right."

It was a spring afternoon, the sun warm and air sweet with the smell of wildflowers. We hurriedly changed clothes, packed our backpacks with sandwiches, drinks, the Sunday paper, and a book on Hemingway (Chris had a paper due the next day). We drove off toward the bluffs, and Chris parked the car on the side of an obscure dirt road. We started off on a trail through the manzanita bushes and Ponderosa pines, wending our way up the bluff.

"Chris! Do you know where you're going?"

He was way ahead of me on the trail, his slender form stooped with his backpack, blond hair glinting in the sunlight. The trail grew steeper, and the hike turned into a climb. Fortunately the path was well-defined, and before long we reached the top, breathless yet exhilarated.

"There!" Chris turned to me, triumphant. "I thought this was what we'd see!"

I caught my breath. Stretched far below was a vast green meadow with a stream winding through it. Towering above were the glistening snowcapped Three Sisters mountains—Faith, Hope, and Charity—against the clear forever-blue sky. Hawks and eagles soared above. Every day on my way to work, to school, to church, I drove past these bluffs, never dreaming this was behind them.

"Chris . . ."

He was busy spreading out towels on the warm rocks and arranging our lunches so we could have the best view. "Yeah, Mom?" he inquired.

How often had I looked at him—my third son—not seeing all the wonder and beauty? How do you tell your seventeen-year-old son how much you love him? How do you say with heart-stopping realization, "My child, you are almost an adult, and you're wonderful!" Instead I said, "Thanks, honey, for bringing me up here."

We ate our lunches in the sun, and Chris and I talked about the future, his interests, his world. And the painting project that seemed so urgent? Oh, eventually it got done. But the memory of my son talking with me high on a rocky bluff that warm Sunday afternoon is one I will always cherish.

As I listened to Chris and watched the eagles and hawks soaring effortlessly with the wind, I prayed silently, *Lord, let me be like that with You—and in You to live, and move, and have my being.*

Somehow in moments like these, time stands still. The experience becomes part of me, and each person, each interruption adds substance and quality to my life as I see it for what it really is—a gift from the Father's hand. A treasure that fills my house with music and beauty.

In the house of the righteous there is much treasure.

—PROVERBS 15:6

TAKE A FRESH LOOK
INSIDE YOUR HOUSE, YOUR LIFE

꙳ What do the furnishings and decorations of your life say about you? (Both literally and figuratively speaking.)

꙳ How are you using your giftedness to "decorate" your life?

꙳ Read 2 Kings 4. What do you have "in your house" that can be multiplied to nourish others?

꙳ For further study read Psalm 23.

꙳

Lord, I praise You for all the good things that are in my home. They're only temporal things; but they remind me of the lasting, wondrous things that I find in You, my true home. Thank You for the peace and rest You pour over my often-troubled life. Thank You for the nourishment that Your words provide, feeding me at a generous banquet table in a desert place. Thank You for the comfort I find in You and for the true fellowship of others who know You.

I delight in Your beauty, Your mercy, and Your goodness, O Lord. May my life and my home reflect Your gifts to me. In Jesus' name, amen.

꙳

My Personal Reflections

_____

_____

_____

_____

_____

_____

Ten

❧

REMODELING
MY HOUSE

❧

Do not remember the former things, nor consider the things of old.
Behold, I will do a new thing, now it shall spring forth; shall you not
know it? I will even make a road in the wilderness and rivers in the
desert.

—ISAIAH 43:18-19

We've had many special moments in our marriage, but this was not one of them. I was ready to throw the wallpaper tray right at my beloved. It was nearly midnight, and Bill and I were in the upstairs bathroom on the final leg of our remodeling project, trying to paper a room with wallpaper that wasn't coming together. When I'd ordered the paper months before, the blue seashell theme and border were attractive. Now it seemed the pattern was slightly off, and I thought if I never saw a blue seashell again, it would be too soon.

What a mess. Remodeling had seemed like a great idea months before when Bill and I walked through each room, dreaming what we could do. The "cozy" look we liked twelve years earlier with dark beams and wood paneling now seemed dingy and oppressive. We needed a change. We wanted light. We went room by room, dreaming what we could do with white paint, wallpaper, and a lighter carpet and by adding a window. We liked our house—it had good basics and served us well. But with five active children and a never-ending stream of wonderful friends and family, our house was like the Yellow Pages—it got used.

Remodeling a house is dirty work. You have to tear out existing places, often having to redo someone else's work, someone else's mistake. But for a good, strong, durable, and valuable house, it's needed at times. Simply the wear and tear of time and use has an effect. And if you're considering remodeling your house, prepare yourself for surprises—dry rot or places where a drip or leak has caused damage that you don't see when you get started. It's an adventure of sorts.

How like God, I thought a bit later, *to speak to me through even this, the remodeling of my house.* I like my "house," the person God has made me to be. But now at midlife, I too was feeling like the Yellow Pages—very much used. Tattered. Some of my pages felt torn out and frayed. And I didn't want just a patch-job; I wanted new. But new with character, and character comes from the old, from experience.

Not long after we finished our remodeling, I'd spoken to a group and decided to tell how God was "remodeling" my life. After the session an attractive middle-aged woman came to the front of the room to speak to me, clearly angry. "I don't like the word *remodel,*" she said. "It makes me feel like a patched-up old house!" She then went on to describe how a life of unhealthy patterns had brought her unexpected pain.

"Well, I don't like the word either," I admitted, "but I can't think of a better description. I could say *reconstruction* or *renewal,* but the fact is, God is refining the material already here—us. It isn't always easy, being God's workmanship. It can be messy."

It was a mess, but the results were worth it.

TAKING CARE OF MY HOUSE

> *My candle burns at both ends; it will not last the night,*
> *But ah, my foes, and oh, my friends—it gives a lovely light![1]*

—EDNA ST. VINCENT MILLAY

I was on a plane coming back from the Mayo Clinic. It was December 1, my father's birthday, and it was cold and snowy with plane delays and runway closures. I stared off to the frozen north toward Bemidji, a place where my father's parents met and married—a place I'd never been, only heard about. These Swedish immigrants moved to Lignite, North Dakota, where my father and his siblings were born and where his parents were buried, both dying young, leaving their children orphaned. I knew this land had held many memories for him, sweet and sad. My father and his brothers and sisters had moved to Montana as young adults, which became my birthplace.

Sitting ahead of me on the plane was an older gentleman. He had that same open-faced, unpretentious courtliness about him that characterized my father—similar broad shoulders, slightly stooped, white hair. Tears filled my eyes. My father had been dead thirteen years, but suddenly now I was missing him, thinking how good it would be to have him with me, patting me on the knee with his big, weather-worn hand, saying, "Everything's going to be all right."

I leaned my head against the window and stared at the still, frozen Minnesota landscape. The words of the doctor echoed in my mind: "I do not believe you have lupus. Neurologically, organically, you look healthy. We can call what you have fibromyalgia if you need a name, but I believe a lot of your symptoms are caused or exacerbated by stress. You can keep taking medication, or you can go home and take a hard look at your life. Do you have to do so much? Who do you think you are? Superwoman?" The doctor's words were softened by a smile as he added kindly, "It's easier to take pills and have a label for a problem. But I think you're the kind of person who wants to look at your life."

We discussed treatment, stress management, physical therapy, and analgesics, but my mind was whirling. Stress! Who doesn't have stress these days? *I have a good life,* I thought fiercely, defensively. *Just what I've always wanted. Five kids, wonderful husband.* I loved working with magazines, writing columns, speaking occasionally. Being on the local school board. Being involved in my church. Doing prison ministry. I had a great life. It was just . . . so much. So full. So frenetic . . . so . . . empty.

I had always been physically strong, with a lot of energy. I did suffer from Toxic Shock Syndrome at one time, and it seemed that shortly after that, I started falling apart physically and emotionally. My immune system had taken a jolt, and I'd had nearly five years of pain, exhaustion, medical tests, consultations, pain in my joints and chest, depression, numbing fatigue. It started to affect everything I did, everything I was.

My doctor thought I had systemic lupus erythematosus, by evidence of symptoms and blood tests. I tried a variety of medications, some helpful, some with bad side effects. I resigned my position on the school board and tried to slow down, to relax. But numbing pain on the left side of my face finally took me to Mayo Clinic. I remember lying on my back in the clinic after a spinal tap, tears of frustration running down my face as I stared at a blank beige wall. I was so tired of hurting, of being in pain, of being exhausted. A still, small voice from very far away seemed to whisper, "Give it up, Nanc. Just . . . let . . . go."

How do I do that? I wondered. To let go. Let go of what? I didn't know how to let go. I only knew how to pick things up and then hold onto them. But it seemed as if giant forces were now at work, prying my fingers loose, and I had to let go whether I wanted to or not.

On the way home, this question presented itself: *Why do I—*

a follower of Christ—have so much stress that I hurt this much? If indeed His yoke is easy and His burden is light, something does not match up here.

There is much to unite us fellow travelers, I thought, as I looked around the plane. *Our quest for significance . . . our longing to be loved . . . our hopes and dreams . . . our quiet, often unspoken yearning to make a difference somehow in this world, to love in God's name.*

"What are you going to be when you grow up?" This question we pose to our children, and their eyes take on a dreamy, faraway look. (Careful now. Anything is possible.) All I'd ever wanted was what I had—a "house" for God. A place to be married, have children, to love them into the world from this sheltered, loving place. But it wasn't working for me now. Something needed to change.

On that solitary plane ride home to Oregon, I determined that I would go home, look at my life, and try to understand what needed adjusting. I didn't know what; I just knew I wanted to be honest about my life. I had been reading some writings by Douglas Steere, a Quaker, about listening.[2] It occurred to me that I was not listening very well—either to God, to those around me, or to what was going on in my life. But now I was getting a wake-up call. The alarm was ringing, and it was up to me to either answer it or turn it off and ignore it.

> Risk! Risk anything! Care no more for the opinion of others, for those voices. Do the hardest thing on earth for you. Act for yourself! Face the truth.[3]
>
> — KATHERINE MANSFIELD

LISTENING TO LIFE

> *But you desire honesty from the heart, so you can teach me to be wise in my inmost being.*
>
> —PSALM 51:6 NLT

Jesus asked, "Do you not yet perceive nor understand? Is your heart still hardened? Having eyes, do you not see? And having ears, do you not hear?" (Mark 8:17-18). Why is it so difficult to listen? Why should I be afraid of the truth? Jesus said, "And you shall know the truth, and the truth shall make you free" (John 8:32).

The truth seemed to be that I needed to pay attention to the way I was living. As Carol Burnett exclaims in one of her comedy routines, "Wake up and smell the coffee, Melba!" I had a day-timer that organized what I needed to do, but often the "real agenda" did not get put on my calendar. It was time to deal with the real agenda—my life.

Real listening requires a response. Hebrews 2:1 says, "We must give the more earnest heed to the things we have heard." James 1:22 adds, "But be doers of the word, and not hearers only, deceiving yourselves." As I flew home, I determined to respond to this wake-up call, as difficult as it seemed.

OVERSPENDING

> *The world is too much with us; late and soon,*
> *Getting and spending, we lay waste our powers.*[4]
>
> —WILLIAM WORDSWORTH

I wasn't sure where to begin, but I decided a good place to start was to read about stress. As I began to study, I found that not all stress is bad. According to Dr. Louis Kopolow from the Mayo Clinic, we need a certain amount just to keep us on our toes. Stress adds flavor, challenge, and opportunity to life, and it's very personal. What may be relaxing to one person may be stressful to another.

But we live in a stress-filled era. We have too many options, choices. For myself, it was a matter of economics. I had a lot of opportunities to do wonderful things, and I was saying yes to many of these choices. It was like going to a delicious buffet and putting too much on my plate—more than I could handle or needed.

Life is expendable, like a bank account, so says Dr. Hans Selye, noted author on stress. When one keeps adding "stressors" (expenditures)—without making deposits, one eventually runs in the red.[5] It was a simple matter of addition and subtraction. I was adding way too much and not subtracting nearly enough.

According to Delores Curran in *Stress and the Healthy Family,* the research she did among families charting their stress levels showed that four of the top ten stressors had to do with not enough time.[6] "Insufficient couple time," 58 percent of married women and 52 percent of married men; "Insufficient 'me' time," 29 percent married men, 40 percent of married women and 66 percent of single mothers. "Insufficient family play time" and "Overscheduled family calendar." Ms. Curran listed symptoms of highly stressed people:

- A constant sense of urgency, no time to release and relax.
- Tension that underlies and causes sharp words, sibling fighting, misunderstandings.
- A mania to escape—to one's room, car, garage, away.
- A feeling that time is passing too quickly; children are growing up too fast.
- A nagging desire for a simpler life; constant talk about times that were or will be simpler.
- Little "me" or couple time.
- A pervasive sense of guilt for not being and doing everything to and for all the people in our lives—our family, fellow workers, church, and community.
- Highly stressed people tend to seek a place to lay blame (job, school, etc.).

By contrast, stress-effective people tend to seek solutions (budgeting time or prioritizing activities).

MY HOUSE NEEDED ATTENTION

> *Because I was impatient, would not wait,*
> *And thrust my willful hand across Thy threads,*
> *And marred the pattern drawn out for my life,*
> *O Lord, I do repent.*
>
> — SARAH WILLIAMS

I recognized myself in most of these symptoms. I was making far too many withdrawals, with no deposits. In this chapter I want to communicate what I have learned—indeed, am learning, because it never stops—that has literally changed my life. In looking back, choosing this direction of dealing with my lifestyle was absolutely the right thing for me, and I am grateful for that doctor's strong admonishment. God used him to speak truth into my life.

At first it seemed impossible to get a handle on what exactly I should do; but the model that worked for me—that I keep going back to—is from the book of Nehemiah in the Old Testament, the first eight chapters. I read this story over and over, praying for insight for my own project of remodeling.[7]

EIGHT STEPS TO REBUILDING

> *Even so we also should walk in newness of life.*
>
> — ROMANS 6:4

The truths in the first eight chapters of this account of rebuilding spoke to me on a very personal level. It is the story of a man named Nehemiah. His city, Jerusalem, had been leveled, destroyed by the Babylonians (from the region where Baghdad, Iraq, is now). Nehemiah's people had been ravaged and were scattered all over, and the city lay in ruins for many years, its walls and gates broken down.

He grieved over his ruined, destroyed city. In this alien land where Nehemiah lived, he was eventually placed in a responsible position as King Artaxerxes' cupbearer. The king noticed his despondency and asked why he was so troubled. Nehemiah told the king about his destroyed home, and the compassionate king gave Nehemiah leave to go rebuild the city, a seemingly insurmountable task. The king not only gave him leave, but he also gave him access to quarries for stone and to the forests for lumber, and Nehemiah set off to do this enormous task. As he left to go rebuild, he must have felt overwhelmed. Yet he started out.

That's how I felt after I decided I needed to make some changes—overwhelmed. Where do I start?

See the Need

This is the important first step you can take. Nehemiah had to see the devastation, be aware of it. He wept as he saw the loss, the destruction. You cannot solve a problem until you know you have one, see it for what it is. Ask yourself: What is it in my life that I am needing? Where am I out of balance?

I had to see the truth about myself. I had to admit that I was severely out of balance, even though I wasn't doing bad things. Too much of a good thing, as they say, is still too much. This was hard on my pride. I identify with the Shunammite woman—the strong one who took care of everybody else. But it was me now asking for prayer, for help. "It's me, it's me, O Lord, standin' in the need of prayer."

A question that helped me was: When am I most fully alive? I saw that I was crowding out a very important part of myself—the love of beauty, music, time to be creative, time to develop deeper, better relationships, time to just think, to reflect.

This above all: to thine own self be true,
And it must follow, as the night the day,
Thou canst not then be false to any man.[8]

— SHAKESPEARE

I had spent much of my childhood studying piano, reading poetry, journaling. Somehow in the crush of family and ministry, this part of myself—where I am the truest—got steamrollered by deadlines and things I said yes to that were not me. School board issues and administrative responsibilities were absolutely draining me. Some people actually do need big challenges. I heard the late Jean Lush, a noted speaker on women's issues, comment a few years ago that for some women, not living up to their potential was giving them stress. Well—that wasn't my problem. I had plenty of challenges, too many of them over my head. But as I studied and "listened" to my life, I saw that I was severely out of balance.

WHITE SPACE. Not long ago the magazine of which I am editor-at-large underwent a redesign. The consultant recommended a more efficient use of "white space," meaning just that—places on the paper that are blank. If pages are too full of illustration and text—as excellent as they may be—you don't read the text as you should. Effective use of white space sets off the article.

My life—wonderful as it was—was jammed full. I needed "white space!" I needed to have some time for spontaneity. I did not have any days that were blank on the calendar. I rarely cut myself slack, always trying to do several things at once—fold clothes while talking on the phone, working in the car, reading manuscripts in waiting rooms. Every minute had to count for me to feel I was getting things done. As efficient as I learned to be, the problem with this is that I never got through. There was always another deadline, always another project, always something else that I had to do.

If working this hard had been short-term, I might never have found myself going to Mayo Clinic to find out what was wrong with me. But I lived with too much pressure too long, and it took its toll. If I checked the calendar to see if I could add a commitment, and there happened to be nothing on that day, I would accept—not realizing I needed that "white space" to make up for the trip I'd just been on or big writing project that I'd finished. Now my body—along with my house—was sending a strong wake-up call: "Attention, please!"

Do What You Can Do. Just Start.

Nehemiah started by getting a leave of absence from the king to go rebuild the city. *You have to start somewhere.* I started by reading about stress, what causes it, how to deal with it. I went to a stress class. The first thing I did was to start walking. Consistently. I started with two miles three times a week and then worked up to four miles four or five times a week. I tried to choose foods that were good for me. I went to bed at night. This may seem elementary to you, but they were big steps for me! Since my immune system had taken a pounding, I went to the library and researched the immune system and began taking vitamins and doing what I could to build up my body.

I found that I needed to learn how to relax. Even when I was just sitting or supposedly taking time off, I was tense, always thinking of what I had to do next. It is still, to this day, a discipline that I must remember. Relax. So what if I have to speak next week or tomorrow or in one hour? I will prepare the best I can and leave it at that. And take time to relax. I quit carrying my briefcase with me everywhere I went. For years I never went on vacation, even an overnighter, without taking a manuscript to read or a book to work on.

I was tired. I have a T-shirt that described me perfectly: "I am woman. I am invincible. I am tired." I wouldn't think of treating my friends the way I was treating myself. I caught a glimpse of myself in the mirror about this time, and I saw that too-familiar haggard look. The world was too much with me. Pressure was unrelenting, and I had a feeling of suffocation and panic. My head ached frequently, my house was a mess, and I had the uncomfortable feeling that a pack of hounds was after me. I tried to keep up with my family's needs and gave to them the best I could. The one who suffered the most in all of this was me, but my condition was starting to affect those around me, too, and I knew I had to change.

VISIT ALL FOUR ROOMS.   Balance in life is essential. It has been said that we are like houses with four rooms—body, soul, spirit, and mind. For good balance, we should visit all four rooms every day. Jesus said to "love the LORD your God with all your heart, with all your soul, with all your mind, and with all your strength" (Mark 12:30). I was doing my best to love God with my spirit and my mind, but I was not loving Him with my strength— my physical being—nor my soul, the physical and the emotional part of me. I was severely out of balance, and I realized God intends us to love and honor Him with our whole being, not with a disembodied, fractured self.

To begin bringing balance to my life, I took small steps. I started with my reading. I began to balance out the theological and "deep" books with stories, lighter things. I'd never had a hobby, so I began to study local history, poking about in museums and following forgotten dirt roads to see ghost towns. It is healthy to have balance; it brings rest. A good friend of ours who has done high-pressure work for many years shared his secret: He takes mini-vacations, ten- or fifteen-minute breaks. He'll stop to look at something interesting beside the road, walk over to a window and study the sky, notice a bird or something in nature. There were times when he would periodically leave his office, get the broom, and sweep off the front walk. Then he'd go back inside and make executive decisions!

Let Others Take Responsibility

When Nehemiah got to the ruined city, he found out where all the other people had gone, and he drafted their help. "Eliashib, come on up and work on your side of the wall. . . . Where's Jedaiah? This is the section in front of his house; does anybody know where he is? Go get him and put him to work!" It was an amazing accomplishment, and the wall was rebuilt in record time, because everyone pitched in and did his or her share. There was no way Nehemiah could have done it on his own. It was too enormous a task.

I realized I was carrying more than my share. For instance, I announced to the family—our grown-up boys who came home in the summer—that they had to do their own laundry. And if they weren't there for a meal, they needed to fix their own. I enlisted their help in the many details around the house (which admittedly I should have done long ago). But more stressful than the actual work was the mental "baggage" I was picking up, worrying about my children and my husband's health and other things over which I had no control.

These may seem insignificant steps, but it was little things like this that were piling on, adding to my feeling of being overwhelmed. I had to come to the point where I saw that "there is a God, and I ain't it!" I needed to resign from running the universe. I was not in control, so I needed to quit acting like it. I needed to rebuild my section of the wall, not someone else's. It's lonely to claim responsibility for oneself, but it's right. It's healthy. As Mom, I want to rescue my children before they get hurt or experience pain. But this is meddling with a part of the wall that is not mine to fix.

Ask for Help from Professionals, If Needed

Nehemiah called in the professionals to help with the rocks from the walls, different skilled craftsmen to make the job easier. I needed some perspective on my life, so I swallowed my pride and talked to a Christian counselor. I wanted to know: Why was I driving myself so? What was I trying to prove?

It's insightful to note that Nehemiah was a man continually in prayer as he went about the practical task of rebuilding. It was a physical task, but also emotional, political, and spiritual. I, too, prayed for direction and protection in my "quest" to rebuild.

I went to a class on stress. I read books and talked to physical therapists and my physician. They all gave me insight I would never have had on my own. As an unknown writer said: "One of the most insidious temptations that confronts any Christian is to gain applause. It is so easy to temper our actions so as to have the approval of the crowd." The temptation to please and excel were driving me, and I was quite simply working too hard and had became very unbalanced.

Early imprintations are powerful. I was trying to work my way to heaven, nearly getting there prematurely. As the song goes, "O you can't get to heaven on roller skates!" In this process of the "remodeling" of my life (a process that took about two years), I took tentative steps to have deeper, more honest friendships and to ask for prayer more often. Most importantly, I was anointed with oil and prayed for by the pastor and church leaders (James 5:14-16). All of these steps were humbling for me, but it was part of my healing. I see that I was consumed with being good enough, with working to excel to prove my worth. I took Jesus' words to heart: "Look at the birds of the air . . . your heavenly Father feeds them. . . . Consider the lilies of the field, how they grow: they neither toil nor spin. . . . Will He not much more clothe you?" (Matt. 6:26–30).

Need comes not from discovering Christ's all-sufficiency; it comes from stumbling upon our insufficiency. But in this self-congratulating day in which we've come to live, we've congratulated ourselves completely out of spiritual neediness. It is rarely possible to save the "un-needy," since honesty and need are what bring us to Christ in the first place. . . . Spiritual need is rooted in our honesty.[9]

—CALVIN MILLER

Expect Opposition, Setbacks

Nehemiah and his men were attacked by other armies while they were trying to rebuild. Sanballat and other enemies surrounding Jerusalem finally became alarmed when they saw something positive actually happening. Nehemiah resorted to having some men stand by as guards while the rest worked. Some worked with a weapon in one hand and a tool in the other.

The apostle Paul reminds us, "For we do not wrestle against flesh and blood, but against principalities, against powers, against the rulers of the darkness of this age, against spiritual hosts of wickedness in the heavenly places. Therefore take up the whole armor of God, that you may be able to withstand in the evil day, and having done all, to stand" (Eph. 6:12-13). We are in a spiritual battle. There is an enemy of our souls, and he does not want us to be whole, to succeed, to have beautiful, relevant houses.

There may be people around us who become threatened by our "remodeling," perhaps because it reminds them of their own projects they need to deal with. Stay with it, and keep the finished project in mind. Remodeling can seem to take forever, especially when you're living in the house you're remodeling.

When we were remodeling our house, I remember one night coming into my bedroom and almost stepping into a bucket of paint and then moving some Sheetrock before I could crawl into bed. At that moment I just wanted to quit the whole thing. Fortunately, we didn't, and we got the job done. It just took time, and it was messy and frustrating. But stick with it, keep your eyes on the goal, and you will eventually get there!

Rebuild the Wall Before the City

In Nehemiah's day a city without a wall was one without security. The wall was a symbol of the strength of the people's deity. Jerusalem's ruined walls told their enemies, "Our God is impotent, no longer a force to be reckoned with." Nehemiah knew that that wasn't true; it was the people's disobedience that had gotten them where they were; nonetheless, he was grieved for the name of the Lord and His people.

As I look back at that time in my life, I realize that my living without a sense of boundaries was not a credit to the Lord's name. Walls speak to me of boundaries, of hedges, of protecting yourself from the crushing pressures of life. How is your wall? I can't tell you how to build your wall, but for me, I need quiet time. I need "white space" to give me time to read, to study, to have spontaneous times with my family.

For this to happen, I had to take some hard steps. I stepped down from being editor to editor-at-large. I let go of some of my church responsibilities. I stopped saying yes to a lot of things in the school.

You are the steward, the caretaker, of your own life. Life is a crush these days—it most likely isn't something you're doing wrong. There is simply a huge array of things to choose from in this platter called life. Here is a definition to remember. STEWARDSHIP: The conscientious management of things that matter.

Like it or not, you are the gatekeeper of your life. To say yes to some things, you must say no to others. When it comes down to it—perhaps the secret of a successful life is skillful editing. As Shakespeare quoth, "Know thyself," and we can amend it to: "No thyself."

> It is highly dishonorable for a Reasonable Soul to live in so divinely built a mansion as the Body she resides in, altogether unacquainted with the exquisite structure of it.[10]
>
> — ROBERT BOYLE

Just as a house must have a plan, your life must have a design, too; or it will have a haphazard one by default, and your life will be ruled by others' needs and desires rather than by what God is saying to you. I've found in my life that there are so many choices and options. It's not what to say; it's what not to say. Not *what* to do, but more often what *not* to do.

This is a major challenge for me, because I want to say yes to many things, and here is where I have setbacks. But I am learning to plan better, and it does make a difference. Frankly, it would be easier to say no to everything, but I want to say yes to the right things. I find that saying no to things like TV and the radio and letting the answering machine take a message helps me stay true to the "design." This is my real work, my life, paying attention to what's going on. It takes courage and work to understand oneself—but this is essential to good stewardship of the gift God has given us. As Pascal wrote, "We strive continually to adorn and preserve our imaginary self, neglecting the true one."[11]

Nourish Yourself; Reflect on the Process

When the walls were all built, the priests called the people together, and they all stood and listened as the priests read the Scriptures— something the people hadn't heard in many years. The Bible says they stood and wept, and I think it was a cleansing, healing time for them.

I have taken some time to reflect, to look on my life. I found it is important to take time to grieve the losses, to see the patterns, the internal messages I adopted that have shaped my life. Everything has its season, its time. We must be patient and allow our lives to be in time, to have patience with the season. To pay attention to what is going on inside, because it has impact.

I had just seen Andy start back to school. He'd backed out of the driveway, his little beat-up Nissan loaded for another semester at college. I'd hugged and kissed him good-bye and then took off on my walk. I thought, *What is this awful feeling? This agony?* I tried hard to ignore it, to make it go away. *Nothing is wrong,* I thought. *This is ridiculous.* I took some time to stop, to listen. The quiet answer that came was in one word and with certainty: *Grief.*

Andy had just left, and what was worse, he wanted to go. Just as he drove out of the driveway, he rolled down his window. "I love you, Mom!"

I smiled, trying to be cheerful, not too needy. "I love you, too! Drive carefully, and watch out for the other guy."

"I am the other guy," he deadpanned as he backed out of the driveway.

Loss happens every day, in many ways. Grief is a natural part of the seasons of our lives, and we need to recognize it and deal with it. So I shed a few tears; then I blew my nose and finished my walk, reminding myself that I now would have one cleaner bedroom! Thomas à Kempis wrote these words of wisdom centuries ago: "So long as you wear this mortal body, you will be subject to weariness and sadness of heart. When this happens, you will be wise to resort to humble, exterior tasks, and to restore yourself by good works."[12]

It never ceases to surprise me to see what comes out of quietness, of waiting, of searching the hidden places, of placing my life as an open book before God and the purity of His Word. "Your words were

found, and I ate them, and Your word was to me the joy and rejoicing of my heart" (Jer. 15:16). As I journaled through this process
with a consistent study of God's Word, I let my pen be a probe to
those places I never talk about, but are there dominating my mind,
my actions. The ones I spend a lifetime trying to ignore, to compensate for. And then I fed on Scripture that nourished those broken, wounded places, allowing God to heal me.

The discipline comes in coming to terms with our wounds, seeing them in the perspective of God's grace and forgiveness, and
then moving on, weaving them into giftedness. The walls at
Jerusalem had been broken down, and the city lay waste for many
years—a generation, in fact—before it was rebuilt. Wilderness
places may be good places to prepare for ministry, but you don't
want to stay there.

> He who learns must suffer. And even in our sleep pain that cannot
> forget falls drop by drop upon the heart, and in our own despair,
> against our will, comes wisdom to us by the awful grace of God.[13]
>
> —AESCHYLUS

Learn to Celebrate!

After the wall was rebuilt—in record time, fifty-two days—the people had a great party. They had wonderful music and feasting.
Nehemiah told them that the season for weeping was over. It was
now time to celebrate, and he reminded them, "The joy of the Lord
is your strength!" Then he instructed the people to share with those
who were needy.

I am learning to celebrate life. There's something wrong if we're
too busy to live! Have "open house" when you're ready—and invite

folks in for a party. Celebrate, even though your remodeling may not be done yet.

I'm finding that real life, the magic moments, are not on the calendar or on the agenda. Sometimes they are. But often our busy lives crowd out the real essence of life.

I think back to some shining moments . . .

Some of the best times of our marriage have been "stolen" moments, unexpected surprises.

My mother took a walk with me on a late fall day when I was about ten years old, and we gathered fall leaves. Somehow time stood still that day.

On a snowy day school was canceled, and all the kids were home, and we tromped over the fields with a sled and hot chocolate in search of the perfect hill.

This summer (in spite of deadlines!) I climbed a glacier with seven of my good friends, and we slid down the glacier on our bottoms, acting like kids just out of school!

. . . And there will be many more times to celebrate. I just need to look for those moments and remember that I need others to help me celebrate, to fill my house with laughter and joy.

UPKEEP

> *A man builds a fine house; and now he has a master, and a task for life is to furnish, watch, show it, and keep it in repair the rest of his life.*[14]
>
> — RALPH WALDO EMERSON

It is a beautiful golden autumn afternoon. There was a hard frost last night, but the sun is brilliant, making the yellows and golds of the aspens contrast against the blue sky. I walk through my quiet house and notice: The walls need painting again. . . . The countertop in the kitchen has to eventually be replaced. . . . Oops, the wallpaper in the bathroom is peeling. Those pesky blue seashells are at it again.

The maintenance and upkeep on my house never ends. After all, there's a lot of living in this place, and there is simply the matter of wear and tear. Soon I may have to do more projects.

For now, I am grateful to be in good health. Yes, it is a constant maintenance to care for one's temple, to stay in balance. But it has been essential for me to understand my house, to know its vulnerabilities as well as its strengths. My personhood, my "house" is from the Father. It is time to live and enjoy the house, a time for truthtelling and living. I want to love those God has placed in my life with no strings attached. And I want to be kinder to myself, more appreciative of this house that I am, this unique person that God is crafting.

If indeed you have heard Him and have been taught by Him . . . be renewed in the spirit of your mind, and that you put on the new man which was created according to God, in true righteousness and holiness.

— EPHESIANS 4:21-24

CONSIDER THE CONDITION
OF YOUR "HOUSE"

What is the condition of your "house"? If at all possible, plan a personal retreat for a day to meditate on Scripture, pray, and actively listen to what God is saying to you.

Exercises to Help You Rebuild

- Stop tearing yourself down (Rom. 8:1) "no condemnation."
- Consistently meditate on Scriptures that minister to you in the deepest part of your being, your needs.

☞ Get a clear picture of God—a gracious, loving, and compassionate Father, touched by your feelings and infirmities (Isa. 53).

☞ For further study read Psalm 86:11-15; Isaiah 58:11-12; the book of Nehemiah.

☞

Father, I freely admit I need Your wisdom to reorder my life. Show me how to let go—to love without controlling, with tenderness.

May I learn to tell the truth in love, to recognize my own frailties and vulnerabilities that need Your forgiveness and mercy. May I learn as well to celebrate the gifts and strengths You've given me. Teach me to live a life of integrated mercy and truth. In Christ's name, amen.

☞

My Personal Reflections

_____

_____

_____

_____

_____

_____

_____

_____

_____

_____

_____

_____

Eleven

༈

HOUSE
BEAUTIFUL

༈

We shall not cease from exploration
And the end of all our exploring
Will be to arrive where we started
And know the place for the first time.[1]

—T. S. ELIOT

We are defined by certain seasons in our lives. Sometimes we live under the illusion that it will be this way forever. But always we are in transition.

Last night I dreamed I was in that other world. In my dream, I had just awakened, and finally things were normal again. I felt such relief—I was no longer disoriented, walking on a floor that tilted crazy. I was home again.

In my dream, I experienced the seasons one right after the other, like a fast-moving landscape.

SEASONS OF LIFE

SPRING. We are in the middle of Little League, sporadic suppers eaten on the fly. The younger kids play in the wet dirt while the game goes on. We chat with other parents and go out afterwards to Burger King.

SUMMER. Early morning coffee with my husband before he leaves for the office. There are swimming lessons today, a committee meeting at the church for Vacation Bible School teachers, of which I am one. I put on my summer uniform of shorts and a T-shirt.

FALL. The skies are brilliantly clear in the Willamette Valley, a sharp contrast against the yellow and orange oak trees. We do the early morning scramble: Take Jon's science project, Eric's gym shoes, Chris's library books. I strap Andy in the car seat and wipe his runny nose. (Hurry, or we'll be late.) Home to eight loads of laundry and a messy house. Looks like Andy has another ear infection, so I call the doctor's office.

WINTER. Soon it will be Christmas, the best time—magic moments, surprises, excitement building. Forging family traditions, programs, and concerts. In the middle of all this, cleaning the house. Endless meals, sinks full of dishes. Children to train and discipline, to laugh with, often surprising me.

In this world, we don't have much money, but sometimes we do wonderful things—a spontaneous trip to Disneyland. Camping at Diamond Lake. A night in a really nice hotel in Portland. We are all awed over our good fortune and feel really, really rich. In this world I have time for friends and extended family, and we sit with tea and laugh about how things are as we face life in tandem.

The best thing about this world is that I know who I am. I am essential to my children and my husband to make it all work; and most of the time, I am content.

Sometimes when they are all asleep, I sit with my pen and journal and think how it would be if I had taken another road—what might have been. But the hugs, the smiles, the squabbles—all convince me this is it. This is what it's about, being fully human, imperfect sinners in love with God and with each other. My house is mine, and my life—seemingly confined to a wood and stone structure with mundane and holy tasks—is instead defined. Even though these are challenging, even hectic times, I feel needed. My life is defined. It feels as if this is the reason I have been created.

And then I really do wake up. The dream is over. My house is big and quiet, and our teenaged daughter and I are the only ones home as my husband is on a business trip. I, too, have a job with pressure and deadlines, and it is satisfying; besides, there are college bills to pay. But it is a less-defined life than that other one. At times my house is very quiet, and occasionally it's very full with adult children.

Transition is hard for my husband, too, but he doesn't say much. His work has changed from directing a staff of a bustling office to working out of a small office connected to the outside world through E-mail, fax, and occasional business trips. How can I tell him I'm longing to be "home" again but not sure how to be there?

I'm leaving to go on a business trip, but in packing, I have misgivings. I fold a load of laundry. I sit on Amy's bed, reluctant to leave. I don't want to go; I want to stay home. I want to be in my kitchen when our grown-up children come home this weekend, wearing jeans and stirring something on the stove. Instead I'll be in meetings and will be staying in a hotel, wearing suits and heels.

Bill fusses with my luggage, afraid it'll be too heavy and will hurt my shoulder. I forget to put something in my suitcase, and he snaps at me, "Dadgummit!" I should laugh because it sounds so much like his father; instead I cry. "What's wrong?" he asks.

"I don't know. Nothing. Everything."

He says, "Wait. I'm going to take you to the airport." We drive to the airport, and he checks me in, carefully showing me which boarding pass is for what flight, as if I've never flown before. We hold hands, my provider-protector and I, and our love suddenly seems a precious, fragile thing, and we allow ourselves to be true—me needing to lean; him needing to lead. We forgive ourselves for our own needs and share a cup of hot coffee as we sit in the waiting room, planning for when we're together again.

The night before, we'd watched some family videos of a few years ago. What immense changes since then. Our children—so infinitely precious—and we delighted in each one. We weren't perfect parents, but we did our best, loving each stage of their lives, even the tender, awkward years of adolescence. We have had such good times in our house.

> Do not look forward to the changes and chances of this life in fear; rather look to them with full hope that, as they arise, God, whose you are, will deliver you out of them. He is your keeper. He has kept you hitherto. Do you but hold fast to his dear hand, and he will lead you safely through all things; and, when you cannot stand, he will bear you in his arms. Do not look forward to what may happen tomorrow. Our Father will either shield you from suffering, or he will give you strength to bear it.[2]
>
> — ST. FRANCIS DE SALES

Change is difficult—more so for some than for others. Change is difficult for me as I tend to hold on to things, to people. My life is now what I call the "ragged edge." Loss but not loss. It is the place where the family begins spinning off in all directions, physically and emotionally. As Amy passes through adolescence, she is coming to terms with growing up as well as with being adopted into an American family. After a stormy day, Amy and I decided we need to laugh, and so we went to a movie together and had a really good time. Afterward she said, "Mom, sometimes I feel so lost, like my whole world is upside down."

"I know, Amy, I know . . . Me, too."

Near our home run the faint tracks of the Old Santiam Wagon Road. I think of the early settlers and pioneers (most of the women reluctant pioneers), who left their homes and families for new places. Sometimes it was for a better life; sometimes it was not so good, and there were casualties on the way. But deep within them (and still within all of us) is a longing for home—a shadowy dream of what is possible, and we doggedly seek a better place.

The old prophet Jeremiah gave us God's counsel: "Stand in the ways and see, and ask for the old paths, where the good way is, and walk in it; then you will find rest for your souls" (6:16).

Even in constant change, a few things stay the same. Such as, I am still me—that girl from Montana that married that boy from California—and had several children. The girl who dreamed of having a "house for God."

THE JOURNEY HOME

Two months ago I had a birthday—the big one—fifty! Bill knew I was suffering over being this old and told me to save four days to take a trip. It would be a surprise. I was completely unprepared for what my wonderful husband had planned.

When I was a little girl, our family was driving to our cabin on the other side of Glacier Park. It was October, and my parents liked to go up to the cabin after the summer work was done. On the way, though, we encountered an early blizzard, and the highway was closed. We were near an old lodge on the edge of Glacier Park called the Izaak Walton Inn, so my father did the unthinkable: He splurged and booked two rooms to house all of us—my parents, my grandmother, and five of us children. We children were ecstatic, as we rarely stayed in a hotel. Being in this special place with its high ceilings, the massive stone fireplace, the cozy dining room while the storm raged outside was a cherished memory.

I told Bill about this place, and since we'd heard that the Inn had been restored, we thought "someday" we would like to revisit. Bill decided my fiftieth birthday would be the "someday." Since the train stopped in front of the Inn (if there were any passengers), for six months he and his assistant Celeste planned a train trip home to Montana with all of my siblings (except one brother who couldn't make it) and some lifetime friends—there were twenty-nine of us. It was like a traveling *This Is Your Life.* By the time we got to the train station in Portland, I had an inkling that we were going to the Izaak Walton Inn—but to have all those wonderful people show up at the train station was a shock. At first I thought they'd come to see me off. But friends from Chicago? California? Seattle? It took several hours before I quit walking around with a stunned look on my face. What fun we had! We laughed so much. Bill had arranged with the owner of the Inn to provide a delicious birthday dinner, and I tried to thank my friends and family. My heart was full as I thought how blessed I am, and somehow the train trip seemed significant—a journey home.

Home is where we all long to be, even if we're not sure where it is. And yet how strongly I see that my true home is in God. All else changes, passes away, and we must hold loosely to the things of earth, knowing we are His workmanship, His house.

And if we are to be truly His house, what kind of a house will we be? Some holy, stiff, formal dwelling? A broken-down wreck of a place? A house that got designed and decorated twenty years ago and hasn't changed since? Or a sleek, modern contemporary structure that follows explicit decorating rules?

I think, like me, you, too, want to be a "real" home. Warm. Approachable. A place where the heartwood is still snug against the solid foundation—strong and authentic wood, resistant to the decay and insects that continually try to get through.

For your house to be strong and enduring, you must be built on the one true Foundation, the rock Jesus Christ. To have your house built right, you must build according to the Plan, God's Word. You must have strong bearing walls held together with truth and cross-braced by commitment and the support of others.

And for your house to have power—be filled with the Spirit—choose large windows, windows with a good view. Make sure your doors are open to the right things, the right people—and are closed when they need to be. Keep your house clean—and if it needs remodeling, have the courage to see what needs to be done, because if you are engaged in life, your house will need repair and maintenance.

Let there be attractive, pleasing furnishings inside, usable and practical—a house for others, not just a showpiece. It's all right if there are some scars on some of the furniture, reworked and polished until the scars are actually beautiful distress marks that show character tested by time and endurance. After all, you want to be a "safe" place for people—a place of joy and laughter and celebration.

And finally, use the door to your private closet of prayer often. It's the heart of your house, a special place that directs how you manage the rest of your life.

A HOUSE NOT MADE WITH HANDS

For we know that if our earthly house, this tent,
is destroyed, we have a building from God, a house not made
with hands, eternal in the heavens.

—2 CORINTHIANS 5:1

At family gatherings, it was my mother's custom to quote Edgar Guest's poem, "Home." I can still see her in my mind's eye, quoting the poem with her quizzical smile:

> *It takes a heap o' livin' in a house t' make it home,*
> *A heap o' sun an' shadder, an' ye sometimes have t' roam*
> *Afore ye really 'preciate the things ye lef' behind,*
> *An' hunger fer 'em somehow, with 'em allus on yer mind.*[3]

When she got to the phrase, "to grow men—and women—good," she'd look at us, and we children knew without doubt that was what she intended us to be—real men and real women, strong and good.

A few short years after my father died, we realized that the heart-breaking inevitability could no longer be put off. Because of my mother's deteriorating mental condition, my sisters and brothers and I made the difficult decision to place our beautiful little mother in an elder-care home. She still didn't seem old to us, only more and more like a little girl that was lost and confused, slowly being pulled from us by Alzheimer's. Without constant supervision, she would wander away. Now it was our task to close up her place, to parcel out her things. On a hot July afternoon, my sisters and I started with seven big boxes—one for each of us seven children—and began sorting through the pictures, the letters, the keepsakes.

There was no order to any of it. Her confused state of mind was evident by the chaos we found throughout the drawers and closets. As we went through everything, we discovered that for some reason, she had gotten into her box of cherished Christmas decorations and ornaments that she'd collected over the years, and the decorations were strewn throughout her apartment in odd, unexpected places. There were ornaments in the hutch, in a bookcase, in a kitchen drawer. Curiously, she had taken a particular liking to red ribbon (the kind whose ends you curl with scissors), and there were little bits and pieces of it carefully placed on top of a dresser or in a cup in the kitchen.

She had taken old family albums (she would have been horrified had she been in her right mind) and cut out all the pictures. A tintype of Aunt Somebody stared back at us amidst a pile of current school photos of her grandchildren. Her entire apartment was a kaleidoscope of decades of family life, of relationships. It was all a complete jumble, a confusing portrayal of her life. But like an artist's hidden signature, there were flashes of her throughout it. I found an ardent love letter that my father had written to her before they were married, tucked in last month's Safeway circular. Underneath mother's bed in a church bulletin, I found my birth announcement. Little pieces of the puzzle to her life, and in them we'd be reminded of Mother as we'd known her. A desk full of her writings. Her Bible study notes that she'd taught from so many times on the book of Revelation. Her prayer journals, her book of favorite quotations. Her diary, found in a kitchen drawer. The hundreds of letters we'd written her from college, from those early married years, from my sister Janie who'd spent twelve years as a missionary in the Far East.

Then we'd open a drawer and find more red ribbon nestled in with the contents of the drawer. The red ribbon must have seemed pretty, decorative to her. How she loved to celebrate; how she loved surprises and occasions. How she loved to laugh. Although her life held much personal loss, over and over in her journal she would comment, "How wonderful to know the love of Jesus!"

"Crazy!" I laughed, as I found more red ribbon in a bathroom drawer with her hair brushes, tears filling my eyes. "What are you trying to say to us, Mother?" I mused.[4]

Gradually we saw some order take shape. Boxes for each of the seven children. Boxes that would go to the Olson cousins. The Pearson cousins. Boxes for storage. I thought about all the boxes of things, things that represent the eras of our lives. I found a letter Mother wrote to me while I was in college. As usual, it was full of unexpected and ordinary goings-on at the farm, community, and church, mother's dry wit narrating it all. At the very bottom of the letter, like a postscript, she added, "Everyone happy here."

The same month we moved Mother out of her place, I also helped two of my children pack for college; and then our oldest son left for a job in a distant city. Also that month I boxed up my office at *Virtue* magazine. Bill and I had published our last issue as publishers. Changes in my life seemed to be happening at an accelerated, dizzy pace.

SAYING GOOD-BYE

The nearer I approach the end, the plainer I hear around me the immortal symphonies of the worlds which invite me. It is marvelous, yet simple.[5]

—VICTOR HUGO

Eleven months later as I sat by Mother's bed in her new home, I knew she was leaving us. Pictures of her family surrounded her as she lovingly touched them, keeping them close to her, still smiling that same radiant smile that had permeated my entire life.

There was something very familiar about this, I thought. It seemed in many ways like a birth. Pain, uncertainty, travail. Knowing her departure was imminent, yet not knowing when. But even there on that ordinary day while she was dying, there was beauty, comfort, and routine. The sun was shining brilliantly, and I sipped a freshly brewed cup of coffee as I watched her sleep. Through the open window, I heard a family next door having dinner in their backyard and smelled their barbecue.

Moments before, when I had walked into her room, she'd opened her brown eyes with alarm, as she often did after she'd been asleep, worried about the time. "What time is it?" she'd asked. "I have to get going!" A habit after years of catching a quick nap on the couch while dinner was cooking. I helped her to the bathroom—one of the last times she was up. As always, she was glad to see me. She loved having any of her family close by. She loved us fiercely, insatiably. Exhausted by the effort of walking, she sat back on her bed, and I held her upright. She leaned into me, a slight smile on her face, content just to be close. She took a few sips of juice at my coaxing, almost too weak to get the liquid into the straw.

What time is it, *Mother?* I mused. This is the woman that used to awaken my sisters and me by bursting into our room in the morning, inappropriately cheerful (we thought), quoting Benjamin Franklin, "'Dost thou love life? Then do not waste time, for that is the stuff of which life is made!'" We'd groan and roll over, covering our heads with our pillows.

Now she slips into a deep, dreamless sleep again. I ease her thin frame back onto her bed. She seems stiff, unable to get into a comfortable position. There never is a good time for dying. And it's not easy letting her go, even though we pray for her release.

Days seem like years as we keep vigil near her bedside, and we children come and go, watching her decline hourly. In those final days, there were some sweet moments, some smiles, even laughter. But watching her die and trying to make her comfortable as she left us was wrenching. Finally the struggle was over, and time as she knew it—minutes, days, months, years—stopped. Ten 'til five on a Tuesday morning, my sister, who was doing night duty, called me: "Mom's with Jesus." I got there in just a few minutes, knelt by her bed, and cradled her little frame that was still warm but so still and growing cold. I thought of the verses, "We finish our years like a sigh. . . . It is soon cut off, and we fly away. . . . So teach us to number our days, that we may gain a heart of wisdom" (Ps. 90:9, 10, 12).

And so that week we made the trek back to Montana for her final reunion here on earth, and we laid her beside Dad under the headstone that reads, "Till He Comes."[6]

Our son Chris wrote about the long trip home:

The Sun Will Rise

The car drones on. Tires hum like a boring hymn,
wailing an old song of eternity.
The highway stretches straighter,
evaporating into a point.
A mileage marker silently stands at attention,
like a tired soldier.
It's green, and then
it's gone.

The road groans on, moaning in a continuous sigh.
Even this dry summer wind remains unchanged.
An eternal whisper, I think
The giant golden sun drops closer to the waving arms of grain,
short golden stalks,
swaying softly, as if to music.
It seems as if the sun is lying down,
reaching for its bed,
one last time.

The highway bends slightly to the right.

I'm going to a funeral, on the back of a Montana highway.
I think of her, and I feel death's hollow ache,
wrapping its lonely shell around my heart.
But not for long.

I can hear her laughing pleasantly—as if to cheer me—
The sun has touched the swaying stalks of gold,
and begins to sink into the horizon.
My thoughts turn to her again; and I feel death again,
Sharply—

But floods of laughter fill my head,
I hear her laughter,
I see smiles, and I remember
crazy birdcages! Larry Bird, she named her little friend,
and when he died, she buried him
in a butter dish in her backyard.

A butter dish?

I laugh like her, interrupting
the sad groan from the road—

The sun has almost set;
the waving arms of golden grain swallowing
the giant star, quenching its dry golden fire.

And I think of Mrs. Harriet—Gramma P.—
holding life with both hands
and facing the world with a broad, forgiving grin.

And I cannot think of death—I can only dream of sunrise!
I can hardly see the grain;
it has melted itself into a single,
gray line of horizon.

I can hear the moan of the road, and the steady whisper
of the wind,
saying,
"I AM THE LORD. I RESTORE ALL."

I close my eyes and feel the cool wind kiss my face.
"I am the Lord," he whispers patiently, soothingly.

And I know, with the reassurance
of an eternal Father,
the sun will indeed rise.

— CHRISTIAN G. CARMICHAEL

Back home after the funeral, I fussed with my calendar, rescheduling appointments, reexamining commitments. "What time is it? I have to get going." Mother's words echoed in my mind. Going? I supposed I had to "get going," but where? To what? Death reminds me: Life is real. It is a gift from God, and we choose how we spend it.

The parting is so final. We cling to the Blessed Hope, and yet how do we know? To what do we hold, as we stand by the grave of one once a vibrant part of ourselves? Even more difficult to bear— broken and torn relationships, torn by divorce and hardness of heart. Where are the graveyards for broken relationships? The emptiness and silence is at times palpable. We let go because we must. We turn away to life again because we must. We go on, trusting, believing the best we can. Life is busy and full, yet if the past is intertwined with today, we can't help but see the empty places, too, and they add depth to what is here now.

Our hearts are mended as we love others, find comfort in the Word of God, and think about eternity. I think of my mother and my father, as if a sentence is interrupted, and the road ends. And a lovely thing is gone. But I am comforted, knowing they are in the presence of God, where to be is fullness of joy. Our Father who says, "I've engraved you in the palm of my hand; I will not forget you; Who are you to be afraid when you are engraved in the palm of my hand?"

One thing I know for sure—in loving and in losing, I learn better how to love, to love with no strings attached. I remember that everyone has a place in them that is heartbroken, or afraid, or angry, and a simple word of compassion and understanding may be the healing oil that will help bind up the wound.

> *Daughter am I in my mother's house;*
> *But mistress in my own.*[7]
>
> — RUDYARD KIPLING

My mother's death confronted me with my own life, my own mortality. Perhaps you too have been confronted by death. Perhaps you haven't thought about it much at all, and it isn't a reality. It was only after my mother's and father's deaths that I was able to appreciate the scope of their lives. I always thought of my mother as my mentor, my role model. I wanted to be like her. But I see that my life is unique— it is not my mother's, my father's, nor anyone else's. It is mine. And yours is unique to you, too. There may be some familiar themes in your house and mine, but the life God gives each of us is one of a kind.

INSTRUCTIONS TO MY CHILDREN

> *How much better to get wisdom than gold! And to get understanding*
> *is to be chosen rather than silver.*
>
> — PROVERBS 16:16

What I want most is to know that my children—and others following me-may get a good idea or two from my house for their own. Especially which Foundation to choose. As I watch my children leave home one by one, I wonder if they know how much I love them, pray for them? How I yearn for them to have God's best for them? How precious is each one's unique, solitary life. But how does one convey such thoughts to one's children?

My children must build their own houses, even as they look to others for ideas. It is her own house, his own house. And as much as you and I long for our children to live a life of passion for God, they and their God must forge their own relationships. Perhaps it's enough to live the gift of life in front of one's children while your heart is, almost without question, given away, divided among them, and they aren't even aware of it. It is only later, when you watch your own parent stop breathing, leave, that you realize something incredibly precious is gone. (But how can love die? "Many waters cannot quench love." Song of Solomon 8:7)

My mother (like my father) simply outgrew her house. She was moving on to a better house, one not made with hands. And someday, if Jesus does not return first, all of us will leave our earthly homes. "Those who are wise shall shine like the brightness of the firmament, and those who turn many to righteousness like the stars forever and ever" (Dan. 12:3).

Love doesn't die—it comes again to us in surprising and wonderful ways. Just this year Bill and I were blessed to become grandparents to Will, Jon and Brittni's son. A new little person to love who fills our lives with such joy. This season in my life is now taking on greater fulfillment than I could have realized.

A VISION FOR WHAT'S POSSIBLE

We are haunted by an ideal life, and it is because we have within us the beginning and the possibility of it.

−UNKNOWN

"When it's all said and done, has my life made a difference?" It is what we all long for—to know that our "houses" are of lasting significance, that they indeed have value, that they bring joy, purpose. That we were more than just a blip on the screen of eternity as we pass through. All of us long for something we can point to and say, "There. I did that."

The creative drive inside all of us is that spark that is like our Father. It is a good thing. We need to have a vision of what's possible. But sometimes we get stale, lazy. Our expectations of what could be get crushed by life, and we slog along, content to just live in a run-down shack instead of being the work-in-progress, the magnificent dwelling place God intends each of us to be.

There is an old vacant house on a hillside in Portland that I passed often. The house must be at least a hundred years old, and there was a For Sale sign on it for a long time. The house was in serious decay, and I fully expected to drive by one day and see it torn down and the lot cleared for a new one to be built. Imagine my surprise when several months later I drove by to see the old house completely restored, rebuilt. It was beautiful. I stopped the car to make sure it was the same house. Indeed, it was.

It reminded me that our lives—no matter how impossible or run-down—with the touch of the Master's hand, can become new and beautiful once again. Real beauty is in growing to be the person God means me to be, and it is a process. Psalm 84:5 (NIV) says, "Blessed is the man whose strength is in You, whose heart is set on pilgrimage." It seems a contradiction in terms to have your heart set on pilgrimage, set on a movable object—and yet that is the only safe place to have one's heart set. I must keep my heart set on the journey.

> How many loved your moments of glad grace,
> And loved your beauty with love false or true,
> But one man loved the pilgrim soul in you,
> And loved the sorrows of your changing face.[8]

> —WILLIAM BUTLER YEATS

Without vision, Proverbs says, the people perish. My mother dreamed someday of writing a book—a really, good book. She hammered away on a typewriter all her life writing letters to us children and in her spare moments writing drafts of short stories. But the demands of family life—and the fact that her family and church always came first—kept her from writing the book she so longed to write.

I understand her burning desire to write, but I am seeing that writing my book is a poor imitation of what really must happen. God's work is not enshrined in ink and paper, nor in physical buildings, nor in any temporary thing we give our lives to, worthy as these are. Jesus said the real treasure is in the eternal, things we cannot see. He is writing on tablets of flesh; we become "living letters" of His presence as we become more and more like Jesus, full of love, mercy, and truth. He says to us in so many ways, "It is you. Just live and move and have your being in Me. I will build my house. You are My house not made with hands, eternal in the heavens."

King Solomon built a spectacular temple for God, as well as an entire kingdom. No detail was spared. And yet Jesus said, "Consider the lilies of the field . . . they neither toil nor spin; and yet I say to you that even Solomon in all his glory was not arrayed like one of these . . . Will He not much more clothe you?" (Matt. 6:28-30). It is enough to let the Lord build our house the way He will.

Many things are demanded of me, this "house for God" that I am. But my house is eroding. The skylight in my bathroom is merciless as it exposes the crinkles around my eyes. But even in this disconcerting reality, I see the beauty of this gift of my life in its fragility and mortality.

What makes a house, a person beautiful? I maintain it is one's response to life—love and wisdom wins out, or bitterness and hardness take over. Personas and masks are easier to wear when one is young, but with time the "real me" starts to show through the cracks on the veneer. The heartwood has become polished and burnished now with time and seasoning and adds to the beauty of the entire house. Pain, laughter, and joy leave eloquent lines.

HE LIVES WITH ME

Behold, the tabernacle of God is with men.

— REVELATION 21:3

Through it all, He knocks at the door of your heart, my heart, wanting to come in. At the end of David's life, he was disappointed at not being able to build the magnificent temple for God, but God assured him: "I took you from the sheepfold . . . And I have been with you wherever you have gone . . . " (1 Chron. 17:7-8). In your struggle, in your sometimes-disastrous journey, you, David, are the house for God. In your humble and broken heart, God builds His house. God's Word says: "Heaven is My throne, and earth is My footstool. Where is the house that you will build Me? And where is the place of My rest? . . . But on this one will I look: On him who is poor and of a contrite spirit, and who trembles at My word" (Isa. 66:1-2).

Becoming a useful house of wisdom is a process of testing—waiting—studying—listening. But it starts with saying yes to Him. Throw open wide the door of your heart and let Him fully into your life. Don't wait for the perfect time or until you get certain things straightened out. Do it now! It's like finding the red ribbons scattered among Mother's things in her apartment. They symbolize to me the joy Christ can bring when we invite Him in right where we are, even in our mess and confusion and incompleteness. And somehow in spite of ourselves, He makes something beautiful and useful out of our lives.

I'm still in the Carpenter's shop, still His workmanship. But I believe. And with you, I invite Him in right where I am, right now.

SEE THE SCOPE OF YOUR LIFE

   ȼ What do you want your life-message to communicate?

   ȼ How can you keep your heart "set on pilgrimage," and in what specific ways do you need to grow in your life?

   ȼ For further study read Psalm 103:15-18; Proverbs 4:7.

ȼ

Jesus, I kneel in worship before You, King of the universe, King of my heart. Thank You for coming into my world and identifying with my brokenness, my humanity. Thank You for being my eternal home. You set me at Your table spread with delights and celebrate my belonging to You.

Help me never to give up growing in You—to hold fast to the fact that as long as I am on this earth, I will be Your workmanship. Do in me what You must so that You will be at home in me—so at home that when others are near, they recognize Your presence. Amen.

ȼ

My Personal Reflections

_____

_____

_____

_____

_____

_____

_____

_____

NOTES

INTRODUCTION

1. Oswald Chambers, *The Best from All His Books,* vol. 2, ed. Harry Verploegh (Nashville: Oliver-Nelson, 1989), p. 135.

1: THE FOUNDATION

1. Johann Wolfgang von Goethe, *Elective Affinities,* Book I, ch. 9, quoted in *Bartlett's Familiar Quotations,* 16th ed., John Bartlett and Justin Kaplan, eds. (Boston: Little, Brown, 1992).

2. Dag Hammarskjöld, *Markings* (New York: Alfred A. Knopf, 1964), p. 205.

3. Elisha A. Hoffman, in *Hymns of Glorious Praise* (Springfield, Mo.: Gospel Publishing House, 1969), p. 395.

4. T. S. Eliot, *A Dialogue on Dramatic Poetry*, quoted in Bartlett and Kaplan, eds., *Bartlett's*, p. 672.

5. Edward Mote, "The Solid Rock," *Hymns of Glorious Praise*, p. 290.

6. Frank Lloyd Wright, *An Autobiography*, quoted in Bartlett and Kaplan, eds., *Bartlett's*, p. 608.

7. Calvin Miller, *Walking with the Saints* (Nashville: Thomas Nelson Publishers, 1995), p. 15.

8. Edna St. Vincent Millay Boissevain, "Second Fig," from *A Few Figs from Thistles: Poems and Sonnets* (New York: Frank Shay, 1922).

2: MEASURING UP

1. Phillips Brooks in *Treasury of the Christian Faith* (New York: Association Press, 1949), p. 47.

2. John White, *The Fight* (Downers Grove, Ill.: InterVarsity Press, 1979), p. 151.

3. William J. Petersen, *Husbands and Wives* (Carol Stream, Ill.: Tyndale House Publishers, 1983), p. 66.

4. Hugh Elmer Brown in *Treasury of the Christian Faith*, p. 44.

5. Thomas à Kempis, *The Imitation of Christ* in *The Guideposts Treasury of Inspiration* (New York: Doubleday and Company, 1980), p. 147.

6. Walter D. Cavert in *Treasury of the Christian Faith*, p. 42.

3: HEARTWOOD

1. Edna St. Vincent Millay, "Dirge Without Music," copyright 1923, 1951 by Edna St. Vincent Millay and Norma Millay Ellis.

2. Mother Teresa of Calcutta, *The Love of Christ* (New York: Harper & Row Publishers, 1982), p. 113.

3. A. W. Tozer, from *That Incredible Christian*, quoted in *Signposts, A collection of Sayings from A. W. Tozer*, comp. Harry Verploegh (Wheaton, Ill.: Victor Books, 1988), p. 181.

4. Stephen W. Hines, ed., *Words from the Fearless Heart* (Nashville: Thomas Nelson, 1995), p. 100.

5. M. Scott Peck, *In Search of Stones* (New York: Hyperion, 1995), p. 155.

6. Paul Tournier, *A Place for You* (New York: Harper & Row Publishers, 1968), p. 136.

4: FRAMING

1. Dante Alighieri, *Paradiso*, trans. John D. Sinclair, quoted in *Bartlett's Familiar Quotations*, 16th ed., John Bartlett and Justin Kaplan, eds. (Boston: Little, Brown, 1922), p. 126.

2. Viktor E. Frankl, *Man's Search for Meaning* (New York: Simon & Schuster, 1984).

3. Oswald Chambers, *Our Brilliant Heritage*, quoted in Oswald Chambers, *The Best from All His Books*, ed. Harry Verploegh (Nashville: Oliver-Nelson, 1989), p. 97.

4. Richard J. Foster, *Celebration of Discipline* (San Francisco: HarperSanFrancisco, 1978), p. 6.

5. Hannah Whitall Smith, *The Christian's Secret of a Happy Life*, quoted in *Disciplines for the Inner Life*, ed. Bob Benson, Sr., and Michael W. Benson (Nashville: Thomas Nelson, 1989), p. 162.

6. Helen M. Roseveare, *Living Faith* (Minneapolis: Bethany, 1980).

7. Christopher Marlowe, "The Passionate Shepherd to His Love," in *The Works of Christopher Marlowe* (Oxford: Clarendon Press, 1910, 1925), p. 550.

8. George Bernard Shaw, *Getting Married*, quoted in *Bartlett's Familiar Quotations*, 16th ed., John Bartlett and Justin Kaplan, eds. (Boston: Little, Brown, 1992), p. 571.

9. Saint Teresa of Avila, *A Life of Prayer: Classics of Faith & Devotion* (Portland, Ore.: Multnomah Press, 1983), p. 32.

10. Olive Wyon, *Into His Presence: Spiritual Disciplines for the Inner Life*, ed. Ian Bunting (Nashville: Thomas Nelson, 1993), p. 361.

11. Oliver Wendell Holmes, "The Chambered Nautilus" (Boston, New York: Educational Publishing Co., 1914).

12. Oswald Chambers, *God's Workmanship*, in *The Best from All His Books* (Nashville: Oliver-Nelson, 1989), p. 284.

13. James Allen, "As a Man Thinketh," in *The Guideposts Treasury of Inspiration* (New York: Doubleday and Company, 1980), p. 79.

14. Frederick Buechner, *The Sacred Journey* (San Francisco: Harper & Row Publishers, 1982), p. 58.

5: THE BEARING WALL

1. Phillips Brooks, quoted in *Treasury of the Christian Faith* (New York: Association Press, 1949), p. 136.

2. Oswald Chambers, *My Utmost for His Highest*, quoted in *Disciplines for the Inner Life*, ed. Bob Benson, Sr., and Michael W. Benson (Nashville: Thomas Nelson, 1989), p. 363.

3. Oswald Chambers, *My Utmost for His Highest; NIV* (Westwood, N.J.: Barbour and Company, 1963), p. 137.

4. James Dickey, "Adultery," quoted in *Bartlett's Familiar Quotations*, 16th

ed., John Bartlett and Justin Kaplan, eds. (Boston: Little, Brown, 1992), p. 752.

5.   Charlotte Bronte, *Jane Eyre* (Danbury, Conn.: Grolier, 1969).

6.   Martin Luther, in *5100 Quotations for Speakers & Writers*, ed. Hebert V. Prochnow (Grand Rapids: Baker, 1992), p. 393.

7.   John Cole, *From the Ground Up* (Boston: Atlantic-Little, Brown Books, 1976), p. 62.

8.   Ibid., p. 293.

9.   Dorothy H. Rath, *The Treasure Chest* (New York: HarperCollins, 1995), p. 92.

10. M. Scott Peck, *The Road Less Traveled and Beyond* (New York: Simon & Schuster, 1997), p. 32.

11. Alan Jones, *The Soul's Journey* (New York: HarperCollins, 1995), p. 102.

12. Frank Jackson, *Practical Housebuilding for Practically Everyone* (New York: McGraw Hill Books, 1985), p. 10.

13. A. A. Milne, *The House at Pooh Corner* (New York: E. P. Dutton, 1961), p. 120.

6: INFRASTRUCTURE

1.   Thomas R. Kelly, *A Testament of Devotion*, quoted in *Disciplines for the Inner Life*, ed. Bob Benson, Sr., and Michael W. Benson (Nashville: Thomas Nelson, 1989), p. 77.

2.   Douglas V. Steere, *Gleanings* (Nashville: The Upper Room, 1986), p. 51.

3.   Thomas à Kempis, *The Imitation of Christ* in *The Guideposts Treasury of Inspiration* (New York: Doubleday and Company, 1980).

7: WINDOWS IN MY HOUSE

1.   Thomas Hood, "I remember, I remember," in *The Complete Poetical Works of Thomas Hood*, ed. Walter Jerrold (London: Henry Frowde, 1906), p. 185.

2.   George Herbert, *The Poetical Works of Herbert and Vaughan*, vol. 1 (Boston: Houghton, Osgood and Co., 1879), p. 145.

3.   Angela Morgan, quoted in *The Treasure Chest* (San Francisco: HarperSanFrancisco, 1995) p. 50.

4. Catherine Marshall, *Something More* (Carmel, N.Y.: Guideposts Associates, 1974), pp. 32-33.

5. From "Meditations and Devotions," quoted in Bernard Bangley, *Spiritual Treasure, Paraphrases of Spiritual Classics* (Mahwah, N. J.: Paulist Press, 1985), p. 101.

6. Emily Dickinson, (No. 254) quoted in *Treasure Chest,* p. 122.

7. Mary E. Byrne, "Be Thou My Vision," *Episcopal Hymnal Companion* (Church Hymnal Corporation, 1994), #488.

8. Daniel J. O'Leary, adapted from *Windows of Wonder* (Mahwah, N.J.: Paulist Press, 1991), pp. 3-5.

8: DOORS IN MY HOUSE

1. Evelyn Underhill, *The House of the Soul* and *Concerning the Inner Life*, quoted in *Disciplines for the Inner Life*, ed. Bob Benson, Sr., and Michael W. Benson (Nashville: Thomas Nelson, 1989), p. 34.

2. Thomas Wolfe, in *5100 Quotations for Speakers & Writers,* ed. Hebert V. Prochnow & Hebert V. Prochnow, Jr. (Grand Rapids: Baker Book House, 1992), p. 489.

3. James Weldon Johnson, *The Creation* (New York: Holiday House, 1994), p. 2.

4. Dietrich Bonhoeffer, *Life Together* (San Francisco: HarperSanFrancisco, 1992), p. 113.

5. Augustine of Hippo, *Confessions of St. Augustine*, Book 1, ch. 5 (New York: Penguin Books, 1963).

6. Inscription below Holman Hunt's painting at St. Paul's Cathedral in London.

7. C. S. Lewis, *The Problem of Pain* (New York: Macmillan, 1962), p. 127.

8. Henri J. M. Nouwen, *The Wounded Healer* (New York: Image Books, Doubleday, 1979), p. 38.

9. From "Meditations and Devotions," quoted in Bernard Bangley, *Spiritual Treasure, Paraphrases of Spiritual Classics* (Mahwah, N.J.: Paulist Press, 1985), p. 101.

10. Finis Jennings Dake, *Dake's Annotated Reference Bible (KJV)* (Lawrenceville, Geo.: Dake Bible Sales, 1963), p. 591; (ref. for Ps. 91:1).

11. Henri J. M. Nouwen, *Seeds of Hope: A Henri Nouwen Reader* (New York: Bantam Books, 1989), p. 203.

12. John Donne, from Sermon 80, quoted in *Bartlett's Familiar Quotations*, 16th ed., John Bartlett and Justin Kaplan, eds. (Boston: Little, Brown, 1992), p. 231.

9: DECORATING

1. Clare Cooper Marcus, *House As a Mirror of Self* (Berkeley, Calif.: Conari Press, 1995).

2. Golden rule of *The Beauty of Life*, 1880s (unknown source).

3. Brother Lawrence, *The Practice of the Presence of God*, in *The Guideposts Treasury of Inspiration* (New York: Doubleday and Company, 1980), p. 135.

4. Henri J. M. Nouwen, *A Cry for Mercy* (New York: Doubleday and Company, 1981), p. 174.

5. Frances Cornford, Rupert Brooke; quoted in *Bartlett's Familiar Quotations*, 16th ed., John Bartlett and Justin Kaplan, eds. (Boston: Little, Brown, 1992), p. 661.

10: REMODELING MY HOUSE

1. Edna St. Vincent Millay Boissevain, "First Fig," from *A Few Figs from Thistles: Poems and Sonnets* (New York: Frank Shay, 1922).

2. Douglas V. Steere, *Gleanings* (Nashville: The Upper Room, 1986).

3. Katherine Mansfield, quoted in *The Treasure Chest* (New York: HarperCollins Publishers, 1995), p. 79.

4. William Wordsworth, "Sonnet," in *One Hundred and One Famous Poems* (Chicago: Contemporary Books, 1958), p. 64.

5. Hans Selye, *The Stress of Life* (New York: McGraw-Hill, 1978), especially ch. 17, 18).

6. Delores Curran, *Stress and the Healthy Family* (Minneapolis: Winston Press, 1985), p. 157.

7. Note: If you are going through a "major remodeling" of your life, take some time to study the entire book of Nehemiah in the Old Testament. The book of Ezra is also very helpful, as it details the rebuilding of the temple.

8. Shakespeare, *Hamlet*, quoted in *Bartlett's Familiar Quotations*, 16th ed., John Bartlett and Justin Kaplan, eds. (Boston: Little, Brown, 1992), p. 194.

9. Calvin Miller, *Walking with Saints* (Nashville: Thomas Nelson, 1995), pp. 121-122.

10. Robert Boyle, quoted in Selye, *Stress of Life*, preface.

11. Blaise Pascal, *The Provincial Letters* (New York: Random House, The Modern Library, 1941), p. 55.

12. Thomas à Kempis, quoted in *Treasure Chest*, p. 118.

13. Aeschylus, from *Agamemnon*, quoted in *Bartlett's*, p. 63.

14. Ralph Waldo Emerson, quoted in *Treasure Chest*, p. 93.

11: HOUSE BEAUTIFUL

1. T. S. Eliot, from "Little Gidding," *Four Quartets*, in *Poems for Life* (New York: Touchstone, 1995), p. 26.

2. Saint Francis de Sales, quoted in *The Treasure Chest* (New York: HarperCollins Publishers, 1995), p. 120.

3. Edgar Guest, "Home," #445228 (Chicago: The Reilly and Britton Co., 1916).

4. Nancie Carmichael, adapted from a "Deeper Life" column, *Virtue*, November/December 1992.

5. Victor Hugo, quoted in *5100 Quotations for Speakers & Writers* (Grand Rapids: Baker Book House, 1992), p. 405.

6. Nancie Carmichael, adapted from a "Deeper Life" column, *Virtue*, September/October 1993.

7. Rudyard Kipling, "Our Lady of the Snows," quoted in *Bartlett's Familiar Quotations*, 16th ed., John Bartlett and Justin Kaplan, eds. (Boston: Little, Brown, 1992), p. 592.

8. William Butler Yeats, from "When You Are Old," in *A Poet to His Beloved* (New York: St. Martin's Press, 1985), p. 14.